Memory, Muses, Memoir

Deb Everson Borofka

iUniverse, Inc.
New York   Bloomington

iUniverse books may be ordered through booksellers or by contacting:

iUniverse
1663 Liberty Drive
Bloomington, IN 47403
www.iuniverse.com
1-800-Authors (1-800-288-4677)

ISBN: 978-1-4401-8033-0 (sc)
ISBN: 978-1-4401-8032-3 (ebook)

Printed in the United States of America

iUniverse rev. date: 01/22/10

TABLE OF CONTENTS

Foreword

This book is about how one woman found a way back into writing, and how figures from myth still have the power to animate all these millennia later. As a child, I loved being read fairytales and Bible stories. I found stories created places I could go, and people I could be with who were by turns wise, funny, kind hearted. Small wonder that I grew up wanting to be a writer. My family was poor, and I internalized the value of education from a very young age. I did well in school, and received scholarships for both undergraduate and graduate school. The small liberal arts college I first attended opened doors to worlds I had only read about. After completing my first year, I grew more and more convinced that if a college degree was my brass ring, I'd better not waste it. I was painfully aware that writing alone would not provide the kind of financial security I was so sure I needed. Growing up in poverty did not make an artist's garret very attractive.

I shut the door on my aspirations to write with resignation born of practicality. Off I went to make the best of what I had. I completed a graduate program in Speech Language Pathology and launched into the next eighteen years of my life, working with children who had language and learning disorders, brain injuries, reading and writing deficits. The work was so consuming, I rarely made time even to read for pleasure. The myth of being a woman raised in the "You can have it all" generation was battered and no longer floating me. Work was demanding, and no matter how much I gave to the children with whom I worked, it was never enough. The birth of our first child initiated me into a new phase of life as a woman, and I felt deeply ambivalent about working full time and raising a child. My husband was experiencing success with his writing career and his newly tenured teaching position. I pushed forward and decided to open my own private practice so that I could have more flexibility to be with our family.

Like many women before me, after the birth of my second child, I pursued therapy for depression. Dreams flooded my nights. I felt increasing curiosity about the stories and images that emerged in dreams. They were unlike any stories I'd ever read and I wanted to learn more. The saying goes that when the student is ready a teacher appears, and as usual for me, my teacher came between covers, printed on paper. This time it was Carl Jung and the field of Depth Psychology. I read *Man and His Symbols*, *Memories, Dreams, Reflections*, *The Undiscovered Self*, and *C.G. Jung Speaking: Interviews and Encounters*, in a matter of weeks. I was particularly intrigued by his work with dreams. I realized there was gold to be mined in even those dream images which had previously awakened me in terror. I was introduced to the concept of the *archetypes*, figures that came forward in my dreams, figures that were part of my psychological heritage. I was comforted to learn that images which visited me had likely also visited my ancestors in their dreams.

In one dream, I found myself met by a beautiful orca, mourning the death of a mother whale with my daughters, and then holding a strange new baby on my belly. I felt as if I had been initiated into a 'different way of seeing.' These images provided me with new energy and curiosities, but what did they mean?

In early July of 1995 I had the following dream:

I'm in a forest. It is a desolate place. It doesn't feel green or alive or beautiful. I feel as if I'm lost, can't find my way. I'm dressed in a long skirt, bulky, tattered. I look grimy. I notice a woman coming toward me. She is squat, unattractive, also in rags. On the ground I see a lap top computer and a big thick black book which I take to be a bible. I think they are useless in our current circumstances. I am aware I need to urinate. I begin to look for a place to pee, but there are no toilets out here. Finally I can't hold it any longer. I begin to urinate on the ground and it splashes and spatters my clothing with dirt and urine. I pee and pee and pee. The old woman now with me says, "It's amazing how long some people can hold it."

I realize something is under my feet, buried in the dirt. I can make out beams of dark grained wood emerging. They seem to be corners or beams of a structure buried below, now barely surfacing through the dirt. The ground around is now bare dirt, though many leaves have fallen upon it. I know I'm supposed to be here, though I still don't know where I am.

The dream was so vivid I could recall it clearly for several months afterwards. I had no idea what it meant at the time. I remember being mostly disturbed by the dirt and grime of it, by the ugly old woman, puzzled by her words. Then as fate would time it, I attended a seminar on Dream Tending. Again a teacher appeared; someone who had the eyes and ears for both poetry and science. I began to entertain images from my dreams, speak to them, and to give them time by recording their stories. Journaling dreams was the first form my writing found. I went on to complete a six month course in Dream Tending with Stephen Aizenstat. In this small group experience, I learned to find the story lines in my dreams and to 'tend' the images. I learned from Jung that psyche is realized in image, and from Aizenstat that giving physical form to the images was important as a way to further experience and actually develop relationship with the symbols psyche presented. It was the beginning of working in relationship to images as living beings, and I found that by participating in this dimension of reality my inner thirst was satisfied. I had been so embedded in a world of ideas about words and the acquisition of language, that image had become marginalized. It felt as if channels in my mind, dried up by years of non use, were now cracking open from the inside out and coursing with fresh water.

I remained in the grip of this dream in the forest. The reverie and meditation yielded new energy. I shopped for a laptop computer for myself, knowing it was truly time for me to begin writing. At the time I had the dream, the only computer I used was the one at my office, dedicated solely to running educational programs for the children with whom I worked. Psyche knew I would write, and that I would need to find the right tool to begin. It was true I had felt as if I were lost in this current place in my life. There had been no outlet for my "creative juices"; I had been holding them for a long time, a dozen years or more. The dream showed me very clearly that I still had the desire and force to bring the act of writing back and into my life. To have the old woman acknowledge how long I had been waiting to release all of this pent up energy made me feel seen and supported. I began writing in the evenings after my daughters were in bed, often until midnight, even though I was still running my private practice full time and juggling the usual complications of house work and the children's schedules. Like Orual in *Till we Have Faces*, I was "with book," possessed with setting down the events which had shaped my life. I had determined I would write my own story, so my own daughters and their daughters would have a record of a woman in their bloodline who had walked through fires and still loved with an open heart. I ached for lack of those stories from my mother line; there were so few. I turned to books with contemporary women's voices to mentor me through these unknown passages. I came to realize, it wasn't just my own mother line that had been silent, but that they were a thread woven in a much larger fabric of women's nameless, faceless silence. I knew then that I would be the one to break the silence, and that the next chapter of my life would be about giving voice to what it was to be a woman. I found focus with my writing that had heretofore been vague. I would write my story, and it would not be fiction; it would be memoir as close to the bone as I could write it.

The dream image of the big black book bothered me. I had the uncomfortable impression it was a Bible of some kind, a book which had left a strong imprint on me from early on. I had been sitting in our Presbyterian Church one Sunday, looking at the stained glass windows, and realizing for the first time, *"There are no women here."* How can I continue to model my life after a spiritual practice that doesn't affirm and give voice to the feminine? The image of the dream bible also suggested the family line, being a book in which dates of family history are recorded. We had actually received such a family bible from my mother on the occasion of our wedding day. I had recorded names and dates in it, saved the missives from my grandparents' funerals between its pages. But the words within no longer offered direction or comfort. Why would psyche give me such an image? It keeps peeling back, to this day. There is something about writing personal story that is spiritual to me, and I hold it as sacred. I am continually humbled at the gift of not one but two daughters, and have come to think of my writing as not only content I want to pass on to them, but also as a model of leading an examined life. I was just beginning to recover from being what Maureen Murdock has labeled being a "daughter of the father," with my focus on doing and achieving, being the best at my vocation, gaining respect from my peers. I was only just becoming aware of how deeply I had devalued the feminine in my life and what it had cost me. I was just beginning to understand the gift of being part of a sisterhood that has existed from time out of mind, part of the community of the Feminine. I was forty-one years old at the time, and just beginning to understand what it meant to be a woman.

I realized that writing my life story didn't need to be about going out to conquer the world as much as it needed to tell about getting to know myself. At first ambiguous and strange, I found the images from my dream offered a new vision, a new myth for my mid-life; that of memoirist and storyteller. Now the words of the old woman make me smile, because it is amazing how long some people can hold it. In Christine Downing's words,

> The discovery of a mythical pattern that in some way one feels is connected to one's own life deepens one's self understanding. At the same time, the discovery of the personal significance of a mythic pattern enhances our understanding of the myth and its variations. Appreciation of the connection between a myth and my life seems simultaneously to make me more attuned to the myth's unity and to help me understand how moments in my life which might seem accidental or fragmentary belong to the whole. [1]

I became more and more curious about myths and what these old stories might have to teach me, and then decided to return to the path of a student and enrolled in a graduate program in Mythological Studies. From the very beginning, the Greek goddess of memory, Mnemosyne, made herself known. While in my previous field of work I had assessed and treated memory as part of the necessary skill set for learning, retaining, and retrieving content, this new path required more metaphorical understanding. In time I would come to learn how the Greeks dealt with psychological phenomena via the figures of their pantheon. Mnemosyne was imagined as one of the Titans, one of the original children of Sky and Earth. She would couple with Zeus and birth the Nine Muses, the feminine guardians of creativity and learning. In her story I began to find reverberations for the writing of memoir, my passion for life stories set to paper.

What follows is an account of the exploration I began some ten years back. I include both information and writing exercises that grew out of my meandering. The material weaves through the contemporary thirst for memoir, the metaphor of Mnemosyne as a kind of mythic image for such writing, how her figure is particularly relevant to memoir writers, and the imaginal, cultural, and physiological benefits of engaging this particular kind of writing. As one of the primary benefits of this more imaginal approach to memoir writing is an increased appreciation for the various ways we can frame our stories, you will find various writing prompts have been woven through out. An appendix of all writing exercises can also be found in the back, along with a suggested reading list. I hope you enjoy musing and following Memory where she takes you!

Chapter One:
Why Memoir?

What is the source of our first suffering?
It lies in the fact that we hesitated to speak.
It was born in the moment
When we accumulated silent things within us.
—Gaston Bachelard, *Water and Dreams*

Stories hold a strong attraction for us, beginning with family stories which nourished our imaginations as children, to the stories of our first loves and of our workplaces, and even to the mid-life urge to become writers of memoir. Memoir is a genre that mirrors both the individual and the larger culture, and as such it serves as a potential source of cultural medicine, providing stories that inform the culture of its heritage and bear witness to the events that shape it, infuse it with shared images, and in so doing keep it vital and healthy. Memoir assures us as readers: "You are not alone." This ability of memoir both to mirror and companion provides possibilities of powerful healing, both personally and collectively. This book is an exploration of memoir and figures from Greek mythology who still offer a rich matrix of metaphors on the topic. You will find writing prompts sprinkled throughout. My hope is the material offered here will offer you new ways into writing your own life stories.

Mnemosyne

Memoir, according to Murdock, is as much the telling of the story as it is "musing" upon it. [2] Such work summons Mnemosyne, the goddess of memory, her daughter Clio, the muse of history, and her grandson Orpheus, the dismembered poet. There is much metaphor in Mnemosyne's story relevant to the memoirist, as each part of her story informs the content, form, and use of memoir. Her presence is encoded in each re-collection, underscoring both the ephemeral and concrete qualities of a memory.

The story of Mnemosyne, along with that of her siblings, is very briefly recounted in Hesiod's *Theogony*. She is one of the twelve Titans, immortal gods, produced by the union of father sky, Ouranos, and mother earth, Gaia. Mnemosyne coupled with Zeus, offspring of her siblings Cronus and Rhea. Together they produced the nine Muses, the feminine guardians of thought, music, poetry, study, and inspiration. She became the grandmother of Orpheus, the lyric singer and renowned player of the lyre. Much of her story, her motivations, and her loyalties must be inferred from her relationships, as there is little actual text in primary sources which give explicit information about her.

Here is her story:
Ouranos was a jealous power and insisted on control. He forced his offspring to remain unborn within their mother's body. Gaia became obsessed with releasing her children and was filled with pain. Finally she persuaded her youngest unborn, Cronus, to aid her in a plan to stop Ouranos from further impregnating her and to allow their offspring to emerge. Cronus was filled with hatred for his overbearing, power-driven father, so when Ouranos came to lie with Gaia that night, Cronus slipped out and sliced off Ouranos' testicles and flung them into the sea. Mnemosyne is the sister who would not forget her mother's pain or her father's behavior. She was held in her mother's womb in close company with all her siblings and their unique potentials. She felt the companionship of each, different as they were, all formed from the union of Earth with Sky. She was aware from her conception of the potential misuse of power by masculine force, as it was her very father who would not allow her to be fully born. Inside her mother's womb she could feel her mother's pain, and she would be the one who would remember. She would not couple with a brother-spouse. She would wait, not interested in taking a mate or procreating. Not until Zeus appeared. Together, they create the Nine Muses.

Mnemosyne's parentage is important; she is born of both the 'matter' of her mother and the 'spirit' of her father. Mnemosyne inherits a connection to matter, both in place and substance; the two can not be separated. Her father's legacy lies within the intangible and elusive quality which often accompanies things remembered. Memories can change shape, depending on time and place, and can be evoked from many different portals. Mnemosyne evokes musing and modes of imagining, that free memories into images. These airy components of memory are the gifts of Ouranos, whom the Greeks imagined as the figure who rises, floats, expands, and is vast and filled with stars. Without the grounding component of earth's matter, Mnemosyne's work would be vaporous and impermanent. Yet it is this very quality of ether that gives memory its ability to evoke and weave associations.

Mnemosyne: Memories live in Matter

a) Think of a treasured/ordinary object; if possible, hold it in your hands and study it for a few minutes. Why have you kept this object? What stories does it hold? If it could speak, what would it say?

b) Ilene Beckerman has done a small sketch book titled *Love, Loss, and What I Wore* in which she explores the memories of pieces of clothing and the stories they each hold/evoke.

c) Try this for yourself. Make a line drawing of a piece of clothing or an outfit from a particular period of your life. Write about it; why was it significant? What about it is clear/fuzzy in your mind now? What happened to it?

d) Open a desk/kitchen/dresser drawer; list the objects you find. What stories live here, juxtaposed with one another?

Since Mnemosyne holds the memory of her mother's painful repressed pregnancies, she is not willing to be a vulnerable conjugal partner. In Ovid's telling, she is seduced by Zeus disguised as a shepherd,[3] perhaps the only way she could ever consent to taking a lover. Her union with Zeus is reported in the *Theogony*, though there is no mention of how and why they part. They couple for nine consecutive nights, and birth an equal number of offspring. The story implies a profound depth of attraction, energy, and fertility. The passion between Mnemosyne and Zeus is magnified by the number nine. In numerology, nine is characterized as the number of completion, a triple three which underscores the three worlds of the physical, the intellectual, and the spiritual.[4] The strength and quality of their attraction to one another is further demonstrated through the fruitfulness of their union. Mnemosyne gives birth to nine daughters, one for each night of their lovemaking. That her offspring are all female exemplifies the Greeks notion of boundless female fertility, as was fitting for a daughter of Gaia.

The archetypal feminine is personified in Mnemosyne. She demonstrates the receptive, creative, and relational aspects of self. Archetypal psychologist Ginette Paris characterizes Mnemosyne as "a voice, the voice of an oral culture, a female voice, a soul voice."[5] Being deeply rooted in the feminine qualities of her own mother, Mnemosyne continues to demonstrate aspects of the feminine in the conception and birthing of her own daughters. They represent both the wisdom and ordering principles of their father and the beauty and grounded-ness of their mother. Mnemosyne sends more of her mother into the world of humans through the gift of her daughters, "… lovers, all nine, of feasts and enchanting song," according to Hesiod.[6]

During the classical period, each of the Muses gradually came to be ascribed a particular area of authority: Calliope inspired epic poetry, Clio presided over history, Polyhymnia's area was mime, Euterpe's the flute, Terpsichore blessed light verse and dance, Erato's domain was lyric choral poetry, Melpomene presided over tragedy, Thalia over comedy, and Urania the study of the stars. There is no cycle of stories focused on the Muses themselves, yet, they were invoked at all the great celebrations held by the gods. All nine were present at Achilles' funeral as recounted by Homer in *The Odyssey.* The Muses gift both the gods and humankind with beautiful words, music, and healing of grief. Mnemosyne's intention, it seems, is to find the patterns inherent in matter, bring them into the world through the arts, and in the process of recollection and creation, restore what has been wounded. She is the mother of musing; encouraging recollection of experience, consideration of metaphor and association, evoking further reminiscences, processing fragments of sensory input. Through sight, touch, taste, sound, and smell, Mnemosyne works her magic. Her daughters have been invoked at the outset of great stories and performances in order that the words, poems, songs, and dramas will be blessed and find their mark in the hearts and minds of those who listen. John Carey suggests that it, "is through the Muses that the outer world is humanized, endowed with meaning and with spirit: through them that it is made real for us and so in a sense, through them that it is real at all."[7]

The last fragment of Mnemosyne's story names her as the grandmother of Orpheus, the child of her daughter Calliope and the river god, Oeager. Orpheus becomes a gifted singer and musician who the Greeks described as a musician so skilled that he was able to tame wild beasts, cause plants and trees to bow down, and able to calm the wildest of human hearts. He is eventually set upon by frenzied followers, and his broken body parts thrown into the sea. His story with its powerful symbolism and theme of dismemberment, demonstrates Mnemosyne at work. Goddess Memory reminds us that it is through the processes of fragmentation, re-construction, re-membering that the call to wholeness is evoked within the soul. Some authors actually link Orpheus as ancestor to Homer and Hesiod. If thought of in this manner, then Mnemosyne is at work in the direct lineage of story tellers, historians, memoirists.

In summary, the myth of Mnemosyne, seen only briefly in ancient texts, would indicate both the elemental and eternal quality of memory as well as its dependence on relationship. She is the daughter of the earth and sky, and as such, manifests the elements. She is grounded yet boundless, inherent in matter, infused with the invisible lightness of air. She is elemental in nature and cannot be separated from the world or life in the present moment. Her story indicates the importance of relationships: she is a daughter, a lover, a mother, and a grandmother. Mnemosyne continues in the world because matter itself continues, mirroring and reverberating the music of the spheres, insisting that the dance of spirit and matter play on and on.

Mnemosyne is always seen in context of relationship, an important detail in my estimation, as memories are bound up in our perceptions of relationship to people, places, and events of our lives. In Ovid's telling, Mnemosyne is seduced by Zeus in the guise of a shepherd. If this view of the story is taken, the Titaness Mnemosyne is just another female duped by an all powerful male God into a sexual relationship. I prefer to take another imaginal route through Hesiod. Mnemosyne was witness to her mother's agony, and after being held captive within her mother's body, I choose to imagine her daughter as the one who 'would not forget' such pain. I want to see her as the one who chose Zeus, who chose to inspire him, not to contain him. I want to underscore their union as one of passion which gives birth to the combination of creativity woven with order, and how these qualities are given as gifts to humankind through their daughters, The Muses. I want to listen to her voice speaking to us through the ages. I imagine her saying:

I, Mnemosyne

I

I, Mnemosyne, daughter of Ouranos and Gaia, lover of Zeus, mother of the Muses, I am with you still. I am part of each of you sons and daughters of the human race, just as my mother and father are part of me. I am Embodied Reverie. In touch, in matter, in spirit, I am here.

This is the story of my birth. Beautiful Gaia was loved by Ouranos; dense, rich matter yielding to the great, curved sky. She could not refuse him, and he could not resist her. It was meant to be. He craved her warmth and substance; she inhaled his scent and touch. He was a jealous lover and when he realized one of his own children would be his undoing, he forced my mother to hold us all in. He would not allow us to come forth and see the surface of our mother's body, see the rim of the horizon, the evidence of his presence.

My mother groaned in agony. In the end, twelve of us were crowded in her belly. It was dark, we could feel her pain and it became ours. She cried out for release until it seemed we would all surely return to the great black void. My brother, Cronos, became our avenger. One night, when great Ouranos lay again with our mother, she who was desperate with pain, Cronos seized our father, and attacked him with a sickle mother had hidden for this very deed. Cronos sliced off our father's testicles and threw them in the ocean, his seed no longer a threat to Mother's womb.

His cry shook my mother's body. Such rage. Such agony. Her body reverberated, quaked, heaved, and my siblings and I were born. Born of both the blood of spirit and matter. We were left dazed and blinking at the ragged opening from which we burst, and we felt our mother's sobs of relief. Comfort, comfort oh my mother, we will not leave you.

He named us Titans, called us Overreachers, said he would be avenged for this monstrous deed.

II

Cronos and Rhea loved, and from their union Zeus was born. Such a creation! My heart leapt at his sight, even though it was foretold he would be the end of Titans and our ways. His eyes were kind, his bearing regal, I did not resist his advances. He caressed my face, touched my hair, called me beautiful. His arms were strong, his breath sweet. I swooned like my mother before me, even though I knew the danger of giving over my body. I have not forgotten my father's cruelty. I will not be like mother. I will not be overpowered with desire beyond reason.

We lay together, nine nights in a row. I am a Titan, one of the first born to the God of Sky and Goddess Earth; I can not be bound to any mate. I am immortal, older than even Zeus could know. He had much yet to accomplish. Olympus was new. He was a royal leader, a father of many yet to come. A model of justice, power, order. I would not keep him from his destiny. We knew deep grace though our time together was brief. I knew much work was in store, both in Olympus and in the world of mortals. Work that only he could do. I could inspire him, but I would not keep him by my side.

Our union brought forth daughters. Nine of them, one for each night, sweet remembrances. I know now they are the reason I was pushed from my mother's womb. Gaia can be proud and know her presence lives on, transmuted and transformed yet again. We called them the Muses, and they are our gifts to you children of the human race. They bring all music and thought, grace and things pleasing to the senses. Even their names bring pleasure. Listen.

Calliope, Clio, Euterpe, Melpomene, Terpsichore, Erato, Polyhymnia, Urania, Thalia.

Each time there is music, poetry, drama, dance, history, study of the stars, they are present.

They gift wonder, light, and joy to all in their presence and are an everlasting reminder of the passionate love from which they were born. Our sweet, sweet daughters. They are your gentle guides if you but take a moment to listen with your hearts.

III

It is I who evoke your attention when you smell bread, freshly baked. You see your mother in the kitchen, buttering the loaf tops, wringing out a white cotton dish towel to lay over the tops, to keep the moisture in. You stand transfixed for a moment, amazed that a simple scent could take you so far back in time and to another place.

It is I who show you your grandmother's face, who bring her voice to your ear when you see the intense yellow gold swirl in a bowl of lemon chiffon. She is there with you as you grate the lemon, its tart fragrance escaping with each pass over the grater. She is there because of me. I weave with your senses and call back events which shape you. Even in you dreams. Your present is filled with all things past and of the moment, I am She who gives you glimpses. I am ever changing, shape shifting the perspectives you consider.

With the taste of strong coffee on your tongue, it is I who wing you back to your first cup at fifteen, with a family whose language you struggled to learn. You see the parent's eager faces and the shy glances of the brothers. You feel the heat of the summer's day on your arms and remember coffee like this is always better when there is something sweet to follow it. That day it was a raspberry layer cake. You turned sixteen that day, half a world away from the backwoods of Clackamas County.

With the flutter of your daughter's eyelashes on your cheek, I evoke your Uncle, your father's youngest brother, who used to tickle you and play his 45's on an old record player in the attic so you could dance to The Giant Purple People Eater. It is I who insist on telling stories, that the traces of your life will be passed down to your children, so that they will know someone has been here before them, and that they are not alone.

It is I, Mnemosyne, who prompts your reverie. I live within your body, just as I lived within my mother's. Matter, mater, mother. I flit within your mind, like the breeze of my father sky. I am embedded in the stuff of life, and in the vague recognition of familiarity. I am both the earth and a vapor, my parent's child. I am Embodied Reverie, in matter and in spirit. I am here.

Senses and Reveries

Try engaging Mnemosyne with your own senses. Our senses can often trigger powerful memories. Try it for yourself by completing each of the following phrases:

With the sight of …
With the sound of…
With the taste of…
With the scent of…
With the touch of…

Now write a page on each. If you discover you have more, keep going!

I undertook the challenge of setting memory to paper in my late thirties. My writing was initially for my daughters; I wanted to give them the story of their motherline, stories about the women from whom they had emerged. I had felt the lack of these women's voices all my life and I wanted to give them something to fill this void. In the process of retrieving memories, I realized that I would have to begin with myself. I couldn't tell the stories of the women of my lineage with their voices; I would have to use my own words, tell my own stories, knowing the stories of the motherline would be in the background, as in a pointillist painting. The pointillist's approach was to suggest form through placement of small dots of color on the canvas. The effect is to make the shapes increasingly visible with an increased distance. I would not be able to view the dots of color from my own ancestor women up close; I would have to hope they would emerge in the composition of my writing, that they would be the form from which my own stories emerged. I had a strong sense of wanting to break the cycle of forgetting, memory's dialectic. So much pain and grief had been unspoken by the women in my line that, by the time I arrived, my own grandmother and mother had become numb to their experiences. Their numbness led to my own wounding through sexual abuse. I wanted not only to break the cycle of abuse, but to understand more fully how the events of my life came to shape who I am and thereby be able to give my daughters a better sense of the dark beauty of their ancestor women. I wanted to stop the haunted forgetting, to allow those who come after me to know the stories, especially the painful ones, so that they might better understand how one can come not only to survive but to thrive in the aftermath of the wounds life visits on us.

When stories are forgotten, they become ghostlike, unnamable. The act of forgetting tells its own difficult story. We are left to search images Freud called 'screen memories.' We are often compelled to search for what seems to not exist. These gaps of 'no memory' require us to read what the stories did not say, to piece together the context which created the silence. It is painstaking work, trying to locate the stories behind the no-stories. I have spent much of my life trying to get a glimpse of them to better understand myself. Through the vehicle of memoir, I imagine making a gift, a visible portrait, to the motherline, one that extends back to my mother and grandmothers and forward to my daughters and their daughters.

Are there stories that ought not be told? This is a difficult question. We want and need to hear the stories that reflect our lives. Life is not easy. Sometimes experiences are painful; people disappoint us, bad things happen, illness or injury can cause debilitating hardships. When a writer chooses to tell these kinds of stories, they provide affirmation and validation of personal experience, offering a way of valuing one's unique window on the world. If we walk on the earth, we will all experience trauma at one time or another. Trauma by its very nature creates pain which is often repressed. Repressions may manifest as persistent symptoms, both physical and emotional. At the turn of the Twentieth century, Freud offered a means of coping with trauma by proposing his notion of the 'talking cure'; a working through of repressed memories by means of free association and construction of personal narratives. It is my contention that the process of writing can also prove to be a healing experience for both the individual writer and the audience of readers. There may be stories which are difficult to tell and difficult to hear, but until they are articulated, an individual may remain caught in traumatic memories, unable to move forward, haunted by what Susan Henke describes as "the ghosts of psychic fragmentation."[8]

The Lure of Memoir

The genre of memoir has enjoyed a remarkable surge in American culture in the last twenty five years or so. Personal stories have been rehearsed and reported in vivid detail, since, as William Zinsser writes, "Everyone has a story to tell and everyone is telling it." [9] It seems as if the American appetite cannot get enough of dysfunction and sordid details; the more outrageous the story, the more likely it will do well in the media—both in print and on television talk shows. The most private traumas of ordinary people are aired in popular media. It is not uncommon to check the topics of daily talk shows and find myriad topics designed to shock: "Daughters Who Sleep With Their Mothers' Lovers," "Mothers Who Sleep With Their Daughters' Boyfriends," "Men Who Wear Their Wives' Clothing," "Children Whose Families Have Been Murdered in Front of Them," "People Who Shoplift and Teach Their Children to Steal." There seems to be no subject which is taboo, too horrible to confess in front of cameras or to put in print. It is as if contemporary American culture has found a way paradoxically both to purge and to entertain themselves through the telling of dark personal stories.

This desire for drama, for details of harrowing life experiences, has everything to do with our need for catharsis. Like the ancient Greeks, contemporary Americans are drawn to such stories, demonstrating the desire for the same sort of psychological cleansing provided by the plays presented in ancient times for the general populace. In addition to the appetite for the sensational, the surge of memoir's popularity also seems to have something to do with the paradox of narcissism and privacy. As writer Charles Baxter states, "… memory becomes a matter of the private and the public from the moment that any memory is committed to paper. At the same time that we're worried about our memories, we're worried about privacy. Memoirs have a way of focusing both those anxieties."[10] The criticism of narcissism is leveled when a text is perceived as somehow too personal, too telling, serving no function other than divulging a writer's personal struggle, a struggle which may actually cause great anxiety and embarrassment to those mentioned in the pages. Such criticism views memoir as a form of self-indulgence and of vindictive reprisal. Private truths are exposed by writers for many reasons, but once they have been expressed in text, privacy becomes a major issue; who writes what about whom generates questions of permission, as well as of social and moral responsibility. The writing of memoir can turn a private memory into a public event. Sometimes the act of writing will require a betrayal; a possible betrayal of the self, the other in the self, or perhaps of others. This is not to say that a very personal piece of writing can not also be written as a piece of literature that pushes the boundaries of what we expect to read in the form of memoir. Writers either consciously or unconsciously hold a mirror to their life events, and the reader is left to judge the relevance of the events portrayed. The *New York Times* Best Seller list for a time in the late 1990s included Kathryn Harrison's memoir *The Kiss*, a recounting of her incestuous affair with her father when she was a college student. The marketing of her story and its commercialization serve as an example of how private stories are increasingly sensationalized for public consumption.

Crafting one's memoir can include more than revelations of taboo topics tweaked to sell for the mass market. Rather than tabloid fodder, memoir can instead be a process of coming to awareness and shaping a personal myth. It does not require one to become mired in self-pity and victimization, rather it can become a process of crafting a sacred text, or finding what is sacred in a person's life. Memoir does not have to harbor judging or blaming. It offers a vehicle that can acknowledge the facts of our various injuries and experiences of injustice; of our coming from a line of hurt persons, men and women alike; and of our stamina, not just as survivors of cataclysm, but as people who experience deep gratitude for the grace of the present moment.

The charge of narcissism is often leveled against the memoirist. Self-reflection is not highly valued in contemporary American culture, a place dominated by the drive forward, up, and out, a place where constant movement is the norm. An ordinary person who would write memoir can often be viewed as self-indulgent and inflated by those in her daily circle of community. When one reveals that one is engaged in the process of writing memoir, it is not uncommon to hear questions like: "So you must have something really interesting to say, right? I mean, what have you *done*?" The word *memoir* evokes the idea of *memoirs,* the recitation of a person's life events, focusing on significant cultural events or meetings with famous people. By contrast, the idea behind *memoir,* writing mediated by self-reflection that does not necessarily describe a sensational event is viewed with little sympathy or interest. It is easier to make reference to the writer's need for attention: "You know how *she* is." However, memoir writing need not be interpreted as a sign of merely superficial self-absorption, because at its heart, writer Patricia Hampl believes, it is not just "an attempt to find a self, but a world."[11]

Narcissism can be viewed as a threshold, rather than a place of fixed self-obsession. The myth of Narcissus as told by Ovid in *The Metamorphoses* describes a beautiful youth whose future is foretold by a seer, a future of a long life only "… if he does know not himself."[12] His physical beauty attracted the amorous attention of many of his peers, but he remained indifferent to them all. One of the rejected youths eventually called upon the gods for vengeance. Narcissus was cursed to fall in love with the first face he saw, which was his own as he bent over a stream to quench his thirst. He pined away in that very spot on the river bank, desperate with unrequited love for his own reflection. Narcissus realizes he is in love with himself, a love that continues even after he emerges in the underworld. Back on the water bank, a new white blossom grows from the spot where his body had been, a flower named after him. This mythic figure has been equated with self-love of the most shallow kind, a failure to love and honor the Other and paradoxically, the Self. However, the story could also be viewed as one in which Narcissus learns valuable lessons in self reflection. Prior to seeing the water's surface, he had not been able to reciprocate the love of another, but upon glimpsing his reflection, he discovers he is capable of love. His death then becomes a transformation; he has become a flower, a self rooted in nature, giving back fragrance and beauty to those who would now admire him.

The narcissism that can appear as the initial motivation for writing one's story is actually a hunger for a world, one that Hampl believes is perhaps gone or lost, worn down by time itself. Through the act of re-membering, the personal view expands into "the endless and tragic recollection that is history."[13] We find ourselves placed in the context of the webs of our society, culture, and the world itself. One could view the door of narcissism as the entry to a place of discovery. If one chooses to step over the threshold, perspective shifts. Once one comes to understand the many perspectives within a single psyche, it becomes possible to recognize the complexity of all human psyches, and to appreciate how our characters and our stories are bound up with one another.

The issue of privacy is another component in the dance between memory and forgetting. In many families, forgetting was the solution for difficult emotional events; then the forgetting becomes a pattern repeated from one generation to the next. The process of writing exposes previously private stories to a public audience, readers who will not be personally affected by the telling of such stories. The alternative to telling the stories, to writing memoir, is to remain as silent as preceding generations. Words carry history; without words, experience is left un-remembered. We may possess our grandmother's ring or an old apron, but without her words, her stories, we are left with only our own imaginings of her life. This kind of silence is often shielded by the word *privacy*, but it only serves to perpetuate stagnation. One is not seen and heard because one cannot give voice to one's experience, and one cannot give voice to one's experience because one is not recognized or valued as a speaker. The writing of private perspectives to be made public could be viewed as a violence; a violation of strongly held familial and social taboos. To bring to light difficult material of any kind is all too often a violation of family codes of behavior. Such tellings can be seen as acts of violence against our parents, against our siblings, and even against our own children. Yet, we can be compelled out of self-preservation, self-love, love for our families and our ancestors, to do the violence of speaking and writing terrible secrets. Privacy may need to be sacrificed to open the possibility of healing the rift between generations, as well as to create the possibility that things could be different for those who follow us. Writer Deena Metzger thinks we must also love ourselves, for "… without the right to speak what we must speak, the self disappears."[14] We become adamant that our own stories not disappear so as not to become another one of the silent ghosts in the line of the ancestors. Speaking and writing become essential, even as we writers recognize the cost of the hurt our stories may bring on first hearing or reading. Writing can be a kind of hurt which liberates. Violating privacy is a risk one must take to carry the medicine of story to our families and our culture. The writer of memoir not only chooses to make the events of her life public, but her struggle to understand as well. Indeed, as Judith Barrington points out, "Self revelation without analysis or understanding becomes merely an embarrassment to both reader and writer."[15]

The human psyche has a need to make stories of a life and to make a life of stories. Story making becomes a means to grasp the events of our lives and imbue them with personal and perhaps archetypal meaning. Archetypal psychologist James Hillman makes the point that we humans have the need to historicize, to make personal the events of memory. We re-member events, putting the fragments of experience together, constructing a story. One begins the construction of memoir with the shards of images, slowly re-membering and re-constructing the essential feelings and experiences, until there is a coherent narrative which feels "true." One becomes conscious of trying to convey not just a series of verbal photographs or sensory collages, but to evoke the emotional tone of the situations. Hampl recognizes the interrelatedness of image and emotion: "Memoir seeks a permanent home for feeling and image, a habitation where they both can live in harmony."[16] Hillman further points out that memory must be cured of its notion of itself as history, that memory recognize its remembrances as images, and through musing and imagining memories are freed into images. Ultimately, "memory heals into imagination," shedding its preoccupation with literal history and opening to the possibilities into the substance from which art emerges. [17] The idea here is to make the move from the event to a *representation* of the event, to value each possible representation as an interpretation that has its own particular value.

From this perspective, a history is necessary but it doesn't necessarily determine what will follow. "Historical necessity means rather we are caught in our stories, the soul's histories, tragedies, comedies, its need to form its subjectivity as history,"[18] rather than being pulled along by some giant historical force before which we are powerless. Here memoir serves as a vehicle for writers to begin with personal history and narrate it through their personal lens, with recognition theirs is one perspective of many. The writer of memoir becomes even more aware that within her or his own unique perspective there are many possible ways of telling that particular story. This awareness of the poly-faceted nature of story, of how a story can be told in many ways and from many perspectives, has been regarded as important for storytellers throughout history. For example, in the African *griot* tradition, each telling of a story was regarded as a particular to the audience and its needs. [19] The griot was an important cultural figure who not only recited a given family's genealogy, but also important stories, songs, and social information. Each recitation was tailored to the individual or group who would receive it. In the same way, memoir shifts the way events are regarded, no longer as purely historical facts, but neither as complete fantasy. It becomes a subtle and complex weaving of the intersection of time, place, relationships, and experiences. Over time we come to realize how our stories choose us, and how we in turn, choose to tell them. Memoir creates an intersection of narration and reflection; one comes to understand that it both presents its story and reflects on the meaning of the story.

Once memory has been healed into imagination, the intersection of myth and memoir can emerge. Moments of trauma are recreated in words, giving the storyteller-writer an opportunity to place them in imagination, a place of creativity. Imagination loves myths, the old stories that stand behind contemporary narratives. Once a person is able to see her personal history and the possibilities of many unique angles from which it can be told, she can come to understand her life as a work of fiction in which she is the protagonist. For Hillman the connection between our life stories and myth is what we all hunger for.

Perhaps our age has gone to analysis not to be loved or get cured, or even to Know Thyself. Perhaps we go to be given a case history, to be told into a soul story and be given a plot to live by. This is the gift of case history, the gift of finding oneself in myth. In myths Gods and humans meet.[20]

Memoir as Personal Myth Making

Maureen Murdock understands memoir as a form of contemporary myth making. She explains that myth is an ordering principal that may help give the memoir coherence. Myth provides the patterns, whereas memoir provides the details.[21] Telling the story allows a person to find the deeper patterns of her or his life, imbuing the present with a deeper significance. Myth gives us an opportunity to view the events of our life through a metaphorical lens, which allows for both macroscopic and microscopic perspectives. The lens of myth brings archetypes, recurrent motifs, into view, each of which has its own inexhaustible associations. Jungian analyst, James Hollis finds it useful to view the word *archetype* as a verb instead of a noun, "The psyche 'archetypes,' or structures, the stuff of daily life into motifs that renders both form and meaning from a life."[22] Myth is viewed as a metaphor for what lies behind the visible, and suggests a perspective on current events of life. Myth offers a way of seeing through events and relationships, a way of enriching our world view. Memoir is related to our impulse to leave a trace of ourselves, a way to cope with our mortality.

Memoir requires a demonstration of some introspection, some evolving awareness of one's actions and choices, and some evidence of how previously hidden aspects of the self become conscious. The writer must work the material of her life, re-collect it through her senses, and attempt a sincere examination of her personal experiences, in light of her own opinions, prejudices, and conscience. Memoir attempts to locate the insight and drama present in the recollected experience, as well relate it to the universal experience of humankind. Murdock believes that "Memory helps us make meaning of our past so that we can live in the present. Myth helps us accept our past and find our future."[23] She goes on to identify four mythic themes that are important for a memoirist as well: "Who am I? How do I make my way? Who is my tribe? Why am I here?"[24] Answering these universal questions builds a sense of connection with the reader who is, consciously or not, asking the same questions. Jill Kerr Conway describes reading memoir as a seemingly magical opportunity of entering another's life which sets us to thinking about our own. [25] We sense we are not alone, that the experiences we live have been shared by others; their traces appear in our own story lines. In memoir, we are given a writer's reflections on his or her experiences, and in the process of reading, we are companioned.

As one writes on selected fragments from one's life, one may find it difficult to go back to the particularities of the situations that were the sites of mortifications. None of us likes pain, and revisiting the sites of the trauma is not easy. However, without specific details, the reader cannot cross over the threshold of the experience of the other. Describing the sinister tone of a stepfather's voice, the crepey bags under his eyes, a mother's emotional dissolution, her hands with nails bitten to the quick, the swings of her mania, eating government-supplied food while living on welfare—such details are necessary.

By conveying the particularity of experience, the memoirist creates an opportunity for healing, both individually and collectively. Memoir becomes a form of history making. It works on a personal level in a process wherein the writer attempts a construction of self, a self trying to gain perspective on the fragments of her own experience. As a result, the writer's larger culture is affected, from the inside out, expanding the very notions of inside and outside. History begins with the individual, as much as with the collective, and how we re-member our experiences contributes to the complex warp and weft of our families, our community, culture, and the larger human community. Each of us chooses to look at history with a particular lens as a construction of events. It only makes sense that the particularities of the individual doing the telling will influence the way stories are recalled and framed. History becomes a shared reality, a common story agreed on by the larger group. It does not spring up overnight in a neutral vacuum, but is rather the product of specific human beings with their own points of view and foci.

Hampl believes that if we refuse to do the work of creating a personal version of the past, someone else will do it for us. [26] The memoirist's work offers a particular view of the world, by opening the doors to understanding those who have lived both similar and completely different lives. Those who experience the similar find themselves companioned; those who experience completely different circumstances are given the opportunity to step over the threshold into another's reality. Memoir's structure, through the lineage of Mnemosyne's daughters, offers the reader another pair of glasses, another way to see the world. It fosters the awareness of the inherent value of multiple viewpoints, and a recognition that the idea of an "objective" viewpoint is merely one more kind of fantasy.

When I first began writing memoir, I focused on the healing of communication between the women in my family, as well as the legacy left for my daughters. The experience of being caged in a house with a pedophile had silenced me, my sisters, and my mother. I wanted a different story for my daughters, though I knew their story was bound up in my own. To make the story, I would have to be the one to forge the links of the story of their motherline. I wanted my daughters to have a story of their women, how lives were injured, how healing happens. Memoir seeks to make the narrative of our lives functional again, to tell our truth about the experiences we have lived through. It is a genre that seeks to bring the pieces of the story together, to sew a quilt of those experiences for ourselves and those who will follow.

In the process of writing, I realized that the story I was creating was as much about recovery of women's voices, beginning with my own, as it was about the formative events of my life put to paper. I now see memoir as work that bears witness: in my case it is witness to women who survive physical and emotional abuse as well as the social, educational, and economic consequences of such injuries. My memoir joins others in affirming every woman who has grown up under such circumstances, and in turn ripples out into our larger culture. Our stories remind us that every person has a story, every person's life is worthy of respect, each of us holds entire worlds within ur psyches.

Myth Questions

Take a moment and answer Murdock's questions of 'mythic themes'.

Try writing two pages per prompt. If you have more, keep going!

- Who am I? : List ten qualities that best describe you. Think of yourself at various ages 5, 10, 15, 21, your current age... Have you been aware of these qualities all along or have specific experiences/ circumstances brought them forward? Which of your qualities is the most public/known to others? Which is the most private/least known? Which is the quality you couldn't you live without?

- How do I make my way? : List a few pivotal moments in your youth/young adulthood that set you on your current path in life. How did/do you support yourself? Who were/ are your closest friends and allies? Who were/are your enemies?

- Who is my tribe? : Describe your family of origin. What geographical location do you most identify with? Is there a line of work, study, or career choice that winds through family generations? Do you strongly identify with those who have preceded you or do see yourself as a maverick or aberration?

- Why am I here? : How do you answer this question for yourself? Does this question even matter to you? Do you rely on institutions or particular communities to help answer this? Is there something you want to pass on to those who will follow? What do you want to be remembered for and why?

Chapter Two:
A Venn Approach

Making Definitions

There are many definitions of what exactly constitutes "autobiography." Some would even argue against formal definitions. Simple consideration of the word's etymology, deriving from a string of Greek roots indicates a deceptively brief definition of 'self-life-writing.' Indeed, as feminist literary scholars Sidonie Smith and Julia Watson ask, "What could be simpler to understand than the act of people writing about what they know best, their own lives? But this apparently simple act is anything but simple, for the writer becomes in the act of writing, both the observing subject and the object of investigation, remembrance, and contemplation." [27] The use of the term *autobiography* appeared in English in a preface to a collection of poems by eighteenth century writer, Ann Yearsly, though Robert Southy is frequently cited by literary critics as the person who popularized the term in 1809.[28] Initially the words *self-biography* and *autobiography* were used synonymously. When considered more deeply, the simple becomes much more complex; the term *autobiography* behaves like a dream image which unfolds in multiple dimensions upon association.

Whereas autobiography is an overarching genre for the story of a life, the French term for "memories," "*les memoirs,*" came into use at roughly the same period. In contemporary American culture, memoir tends to be constructed from particular periods in a life, often characterized by multiple episodes with no coherent plot. What distinguishes *memoir* from *autobiography* is the choice of subject matter; *memoir* requires the writer to select a theme which serves as the template/loom for the work. The writer of memoir attempts both to tell the story of recollected events and to make some kind of meaning of them. Memoir becomes a means of participation in the struggle to apprehend and make sense of the events of a life. The memoirist must be able to convey the particularity of human experience in such a way that it sets off a chord of recognition within the reader.

In terms of literary history, memoir proceeded from the personal essay, though contemporary memoir often also displays the techniques and characteristics of fiction. In memoir, the writer is able to shift time, use flashbacks, re-create dialogue, and move fluidly between depicting scenes and musing over them. The tone of memoir is conversational and reflective, a form which *speaks* intimately to its readers, a form which invites reciprocal musing in the reader. Two principal features of the contemporary memoir—its incremental, episodic structure and its preoccupation with the physicality of a materially located place in history and culture—are present as early as the fifteenth century in the writings of Margery Kemp, a woman recognized as one of first writers of memoir. Kemp's writing focused on her spiritual life and the constant interruptions of worldly demands, particularly the needs of her husband and children. Her writing also demonstrates accessibility of both content and form. Scholar and writer Helen Buss maintains that memoir grew in familiarity as a mode of autobiographical expression as it became more and more accessible

> ... not only because of its use of plain speaking, vernacular language, but also because of its preoccupation with the immediate scene, with the details of individual local and communal history. ... it accommodated itself well to an emphasis on a sense of the writer's self, not as a person free from dependence and community, but always bound by the necessity of community. [29]

Buss continues:

> In the memoir, as in the essay in recent times, writers are examining the construction of their own narrative voice, often through the device of the pointed anecdote, which combines personal concerns with an illustrative scene that

points to broader concerns. This is a process by which the memoirist questions and doubts the remembered past and the remembered self, investigates her own present motivations in relation to the past, presents contradictory voices, suggests alternative ways of thinking, admits her own shifting and even multiple viewpoints and self assessments.[30]

Memoir's dance with objectivity and factualness is one of the reasons it has historically been found in the margins of classification schemes. Memoirs, because of the very nature of their form, admit the limitation of their sources. Because of their dependence on narrators who are never fully impartial, and often highly opinionated, memoirs have been viewed as both bad history (which assumes objectivity) and inferior literature (which prefers narratives that 'show' rather than 'tell').

Writers of life stories may present inconsistent views of themselves, so the readers must judge for themselves what kind of truthfulness is being constructed. Such understandings allow the reader to enter the text with a modified suspension of belief, because they know on some level this story is just one possible construction that the writer chose to tell. The reader understands that what is left *out* of the story is just as important as what *is* recorded and becomes part of the text the author created which reflects the complexity of the life. The reader of life stories must adjust expectations of "truth" when reading such stories, remembering that memoir is a kind of an inter-subjective exchange between narrator and reader, a place where one enters the imaginal field of an other. By shifting the emphasis from assessing/verifying knowledge to observing processes of communicative exchange and understanding, autobiographical narration becomes more slippery, one which doesn't conform to black and white journalistic reports. The reader must come to terms with the inescapable unreliability of autobiography and memoir because the writer can never fully capture her own subjectivity, and the narrative "I" becomes a kind of fictional person. One of my favorite contemporary memoirs which places this notion of truthfulness front and center is Lauren Slater's *Lying*. The opening sentence reads: "I exaggerate." Her way of unfolding this story about illness and health embraces ambiguity and manages to convey a narrator who is engaging and playful, though possibly not entirely trustworthy. We read on because her voice is unique and we want to find out what happens to her.

Literary scholars Sidonie Smith and Julia Watson believe it is important to make distinctions between the terms "life writing," "life narrative," and "autobiography." They define life writing as a general term for writing of diverse kinds that takes life as its subject. Life narrative is viewed as a somewhat narrower term that includes many kinds of self referential writing, including autobiography. Life narrative is described as a form that may "… best be approached as a kind of moving target, a set of ever shifting self referential practices that engage the past in order to reflect on identity in the present."[31] They propose the term *life narration* as one better suited to women's writing. It refers to "a historically situated practice of self representation … in which the authors engage personal experience through personal storytelling."[32] And further, "…autobiographical narrators are the center of their own stories, they assemble historical fragments and are interested in the meaning of larger forces or conditions, events for [the construction of] their own stories."[33] From this perspective, life narrative is not fiction, but is aware of itself as *one version* of events, and the construction generally contains a plot, dialogue, setting, characterization that often blur lines between life narration and the first-person novel. It is important to keep in mind that while life narratives contain "facts," they offer a subjective truth, and as such cannot be reduced to or understood as only a historical record. When we are intent on setting down an event or series of life experiences, we are making a kind of history; one seen through a uniquely personal pair of glasses.

Another approach in situating autobiography is suggested by Janet Varner Gunn, who considers relationship to the text and both moments of reading, "by the autobiographer who, in effect, is reading his or her life; and by the reader of the autobiographical text," who via the text, re-reads her/his own life experiences by analogy.[34] The text of one's life is always being read by the very self who is writing as one recollects the pieces in attempting to make a narrative of the experiences. Autobiography becomes a self construction. For me, the term *memoir* refers to this more focused and thematically shaped autobiographical material. Because this type of re-collection is written more around selected themes and more consciously shaped, it falls within the imaginal realm of Mnemosyne, mother of the Muses.

The Venn Diagram: A Content, Form and Use Model

Given the idea of having "a map of the territory," I have found the multiple lenses of a Venn diagram that depicts content, form, and use as a helpful way to approach memoir. The idea comes from a similar model first demonstrated by psycho-linguists Margaret Lahey and Lois Bloom who were involved in charting the course of human language development. They used this diagram to define language and its components thus: "Language consists of some aspect of content or meaning (semantics) that is coded or represented by linguistic form (syntax) for some purpose or use in a particular context (pragmatics)."[35]

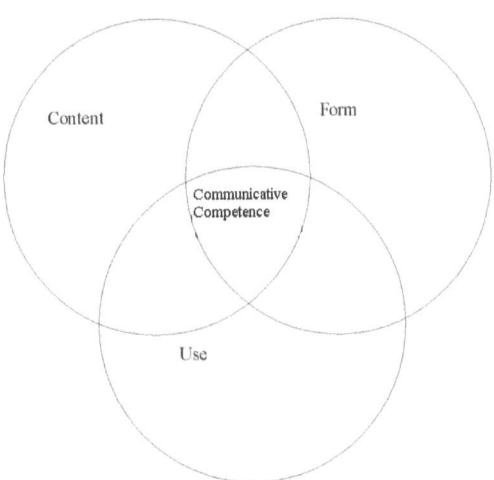

Figure 1

Content is defined as the topics chosen, *form* as the structures of the communication, and *use* as the reasons for its expression. The area in the center, where each circle overlaps the others, represents the shared functions required for true communicative competence, namely, the ability to interact independently and effectively with one's environment.

A more metaphoric version can serve as a way to approach memoir. (Figure 2). Contemporary writers also make choices of content, form, and use. The center of the diagram, the area where these areas overlap, becomes the Imaginal Field of the Other (read: memoirist), or an aperture which opens the reader to the experience of an Other.

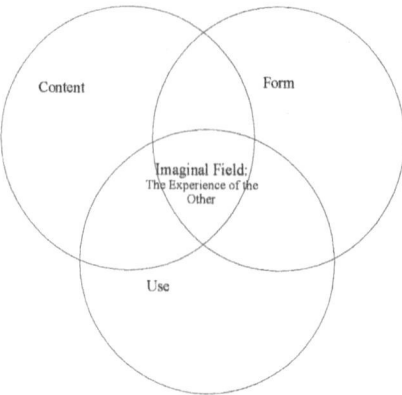

Figure 2

In choosing this model I recognize a preference for circles, for movement, and for intersections. It offers a way to consider the material in a manner that is protean enough to suit the topic of life narratives. The truth is, this idea popped in my mind one morning while I was standing in the shower. I began drawing circles in the steam on the glass. It occurred to me that this model from my former work with language disorders also offered a map for thinking about memoir. I like to think of it as a gift from Memory herself; one way she helped me re-member my work with language, writing, healing and craft.

Considering Content: What are your stories?

Historically men's and women's life stories have been written differently. Estelle Jelinek identifies multiple characteristics which seem to represent women's life stories; *content* with emphasis on personal matters, family, close friends, home and domestic affairs, more nonchronological and disjunctive *forms* with episodic and anecdotal pieces, and a *voice* depicting multi-dimensional and fragmented self-image, a self-image shaded by a sense of being different and/or inadequate. She describes major differences in the subject matter, or content, of women's writing. This is the circle in the Venn diagram that represents content or semantics, the place where meaning is made from both general and particular categories of experience. The parallels here suggest that women's writing demonstrated more topic-focused and episodic material emphasizing personal experience, whereas men's writing of the same periods is more general in overarching content and more comfortable with semantic abstractions. Literary scholar and writer Suzanne Juhasz points out: "Dailiness matters to most women; and dailiness is by definition never a conclusion, always a *process.*"[36] This persistent pattern gives credence to the idea of a female culture, a woman's experience of the world. Women have tended to write about their world; one comprised of family, friends, and issues that are crucial to their survival.

Women's self narratives have tended to de-emphasize professional accomplishments relative to the more personal and emotional matters. Women's stories, Juharz notes, tend to be like their lives—patterned in more repetitive, cyclical, and cumulative structures. Women's life narratives demonstrate a greater reliance on specific details, an interest in how events unfold and how relationships evolve, the content more concerned with process rather than an ultimate point of an event.

Considering Mnemosyne's story, one can see her imprint in women's self writing; she, too, was concerned with remembering the particulars of family relationship, of traumas, and the concrete details of daily life. Because her mother was Gaia, she is imagined as a goddess who lives in matter. Patricia Berry points out that these three words, *matter, mater, mother*, are cognates, related by semantics to the material stuff of life. She points out that "mother" has a primal relationship to matter itself (Gaia), and as such is the creative ground out of which the "new/next" are born. [37] Given Mnemosyne's story, it is not surprising that women's life writing would be focused on the particulars of life experience with an emphasis on personal and familial relationships as well as traumas.

When we think about the content of our personal stories, it is important to realize where we are in the web of things. Each vantage point is unique, particular by virtue of the myriad threads of race, class, gender experiences, and culture. When reading life narratives, we must keep the idea of pluralities of identity within our interpretive framework, remembering that the one writing is never just a 'woman' or 'man.

Content Exercises:

Make a list of the events, people, places that have been important in your life.

Start with ten, try to expand it to twenty, then thirty items.

What has been your 'bottom line' when it has come to choosing which path to follow?

Do you see any patterns, cycles, or nested boxes?

How would you describe your own 'window' on the world?

How has geography, family, friendships, and group affiliation influenced your life?

Complete the phrase:

"I have always... " Write two pages.

"I have never... " Write two pages.

How do I shape my stories?

The *form* of women's life stories has been distinctive when compared to men's. Jelinek has said that disjunctive and discontinuous narrative forms better suit the multi-faceted, fragmented, meandering, and circular experiences common to the lives of women. Her own work emphasizes the historical cultural constraints which initially shaped the range of choices of forms available to women writers: diaries, journals, social calendars, or spiritual explorations.

In the first Venn diagram, the circle of form represents the location for a means of connecting sign —in this case the structural choices a writer makes —with meaning. Historically, much literary criticism of women's life narratives discounted them for not meeting the standards by which the literary canon defined "autobiography."

In 1956, literary critic Richard Lillard listed a variety of techniques of form which he considered outside the realm of autobiography, including flashbacks, anecdotes, reconstructed scenes, dialogue, diary and journal notes, vignettes about ancestors and parents, travel notes, random memories from childhood and youth, dropping names, racing through a story, and disguising events or character qualities.[38] In his attempt to define the genre of autobiography further, Lillard excludes the majority of published women's life writing because they do not possess the correct form.

Unfortunately, even though there are many contemporary critics who disagree with this nearly fifty-year-old list of disqualifying criteria, many literary critics still dismiss women's life narratives from the accepted canon. Jelinek points out that even as late as the 1980s, women's life writings continued to be thought of as not meeting the standards of the genre of autobiography due to their "…episodic and anecdotal nature, their non-progressive narratives, their fragmented forms, their focus on others, and their lack of self assertion, all of which are considered obstacles to the shaping of a 'true' autobiography." [39]

Feminism has encouraged women to instead make specific choices to *break up* narrative, as Helene Cixous describes, to "... take after birds and thieves...to pass through, fly the coop, take pleasure in jumbling the order of space, disorienting it, changing around the furniture, things, values, breaking them up, emptying structures, turning the proper upside down."[40] Such a perspective rejects the notion of women's forms as a "second best" kind of literature just because such forms are different from the established canon. In fact, the scholarship of women in the past two decades has provoked a new push to describe memoir as its own genre. Women have continued describing, defining, re-naming the practice of this kind of life writing in ways that jumble and disorient previously held definitions and boundaries. One such renaming is *life writing*, which is meant to challenge the previous traditional limits of autobiography and include memoir, diaries, letters, journals, and other personally inflected texts. Women's narratives often require the reader to think about connection, dailiness, and emotion work—

elements which have subversive and emancipatory potential for any personal narrative.

Another observation regarding form is made with respect to the narrative voice. Helen Buss describes the memoirist's narrative voice as tri-partite; 1) that of participant— the central protagonist 2) that of witness— the one who observes and records, 3) that of the reflective/reflexive consciousness which, writing from a time distant from the events portrayed, supplies various contexts. [41] All three aspects are necessary for an effective piece of memoir. In the choices of form a woman makes, these three components of voice help a woman craft a memoir rich in circular awareness; she is the heroine, scribe, and student of her own material.

Women have been conscious of cultural disapproval and rejection for writing their life narratives, and as a result the shape of their texts has been influenced. Helen Buss reminds us how women's memoir has played ".... off the confessional form in that it has at its core a desire to reveal the hidden thing, the forbidden knowledge, the shameful and guilty secret, and to make what was formerly a private matter into public knowledge."[42] Women have tried to navigate the territories between silence and trespass by working with a variety of methods—avoiding particular audiences, courting others, engaging in self censorship, creating disguises, apologies and negations.[43] On the other hand, Author Anais Nin noted, "It is feminine to be oblique. This isn't cheating. It's the fear of being judged." [44]

In traveling this potentially dangerous terrain, Judy Long notes three strategies used by women in the form they choose to present their stories; "telling it slant," "telling it straight," and "telling it messy."[45] Each of these strategies becomes a way of coping with possible negative reactions to a woman's writing. The notion of "telling it slant" comes from an Emily Dickinson poem. It calls up the social constraints within which a woman may find herself, and by using disclaimers, negation of self, and denials of affect, a woman writer can avoid a head-on confrontation with the dominant male perspective. Changing the patriarchy will not happen by employing more force; change will happen organically as women infiltrate more and more of the cultural canon. "Telling it slant" is a wily survivor strategy employed by those in a position of less power *vis-à-vis* a more dominant group within the culture, a way of entering by a side door. It is not surprising therefore, that women have taken up memoir as a vehicle for their stories. "Female memoirs retain a discursive, episodic, 'unstructured' character which on the one hand corresponds to the daily experience of women's lives, and on the other deviates from pattern of the inspirational male autobiography." [46] Taking up the very writing of "memoir" is a way to avoid comparison with the established literary genre of autobiography, a way of exploring life narrative without being required to adhere to prescribed features of form and content.

"Telling it slant" is also a dominant mode of the Muses, expressing difficult content with beautiful words and melody lines. As daughters of Mnemosyne, the Muses understand the necessity of remembering war, rape, death, and sadness. The Muses take these difficult themes and choose forms for presentation which allow the culture to absorb them. The imaginal lineage of the Muses is present each time a woman writes her own difficult story, crafting it in language which can be taken in by those who read it. "Telling it slant" is a way for the woman writer to offer the medicine of her voice and experiences to the larger culture which has been made ill through millennium of misogyny.

"Telling it messy" is another way to deflect scrutiny from male critics. Long reiterates earlier observations that women's lives are different from those of their male counterparts, describing how many "...women's lives are messy—they involve dirt, diapers, infections, blood, repetitive labor, interruptions, lack of closure, obligations, intensity, vigilance, minutiae." [47] This kind of telling comes out of the body and echoes the inspiration of the Muses Terpsichore, Erato and Euterpe. Exploration of emotions and expression of feelings are also considered "messy," drawing the reader into writer's interior and providing opportunities to explore similar personal emotional experiences. Finding a form for this "messiness" requires creativity, as traditional autobiographical form assumes a focused trajectory. Women's lives, filled with non-linear experiences of time, webs of relationships, endless process work, diffuse and open organization, and lack of unilateral control, call for varied and unique forms of expression. Memoir's strength is in its elasticity; it is a form which makes room for the many variations and "messiness" within a single woman's life as well the community in which she finds herself.

> Contemporary women's memoirs, while concerned with the life of the individual, are also able to make more general statements about the nature of community life. Through its blending of styles—dramatic, narrative, essayistic, descriptive, imaginistic—and its practice of combining factually based testimony and fictive anecdote, the memoir form bridges the typical strategies of historical and literary discourses in order to establish necessary connections between public and private, personal and political.[48]

Women's memoir celebrates the messiness of life experience and mixes styles of writing so as to more fully capture those experiences in text.

The third narrative strategy employed by women is identified as "telling it straight," harkening back to Clio, muse of history. A simple and direct way to do this is to bring women's voices from the margins into the center of the discussion, including both women's work and lived experiences into view. With respect to women's memoir, this means bringing more women's texts into discussions of the history of written narratives as well as bringing a greater variety of such texts into consideration as exemplars of the genre. Including the stories of women's lives across disciplines and fields of study becomes a way to change expectations and broaden the definitions of both scholarship and memoir itself.

Form Exercises:

Pick a moment from your life after which you knew things would never be the same. Try writing it 'straight', what are the facts; the who, what, when, where, why and how of it. Write it in the third person. Write it as an entry for a 'News About Town/Social Scene' section of the local newspaper.

Take the same event and try writing it 'slant.' What do you imagine it looked like from the perspective of an onlooker? What effect did this experience have on your life?

What do you want others to know about it? Why is it important to tell this story?

Now try writing it 'messy.' Include as many sensory details as you can. What were the emotions of the situation? Use dialogue. Try to let the scene speak for itself.

Why do we write?

The third component of this model for exploring memoir is that of *use*. This is the circle in the Venn diagram which represents pragmatics, the place that situates the "why?" behind the presentation of the stories we chooses to tell.

Although it can be argued that the overarching genre of autobiography is an attempt at a kind of self defense, memoirists have written for a myriad of other reasons. Women often write in order to know themselves better, to explore their most private memories, as well as put forward pleas for understanding and justifications for the choices they have made. Women's self writing within the past two hundred years in America has also been undertaken for the purposes of gaining professional recognition and acceptance from a larger audience. Self writing has been used as a way to propagandize for particular social causes, most notably for women's suffrage. According to literary scholar Kathleen Dehler, the use of life narrative as a kind of "confessional" writing that took as its subject matter the shifts in life perspective became prominent around the time of women's suffrage and again during the second wave of Feminism.[49] Women who came to understand the importance of real participation in political processes felt the urge to communicate with a larger audience to awaken the society/culture to the benefits of a new way of understanding/being. Such writings continue to appear as women strive to articulate the range of ways they have experienced oppression as well as the numerous paths they have taken to new liberations. Confessional writing often seeks to make a case on behalf of the new liberations, whatever they are, from active participation in electoral processes to obtaining advanced educational degrees to participation in social reform movements. Writers within this mode are out to change the reader as they themselves have been changed. Feminist Leigh Gilmore underscores how speaking and writing can become a political act.

> The recurring mark in women's autobiographies can be found in the shared sense that the written record, a testimonial, [. . .] can represent a person, stand in her absence for her truth, can re- member her life. [. . .] writing can be a political act, because it asserts a right to speak rather than be spoken for.[50]

The use of women's life narratives from this vantage point is for participation in political processes, for claiming power, even if the writer has little hope of shifting a negative condition or institution. One voice at a time may be enough to raise awareness to "re-figure the grounds of contention as ideological." [51] Since the second wave of feminism, the style of this kind of writing has moved from the world of external affairs and public life to include also the more particular and daily details of the writer's life. Women are no longer moved to write only as participants and advocates for particular social causes, now they write of the particular and personal elements of their lives out of the recognition that the personal *is* political. Life narratives demonstrate by their very unique characteristics what it is to be a particular woman in a particular place and time. Unlike their predecessors around the turn of the twentieth century, contemporary life narrative writers seem to feel free to include diverse and genre crossing forms including dialogue, characterization, flashbacks, anecdotes, reconstructed scenes, and vignettes of parents and ancestors—all of those techniques once named by Lillard in 1956 as taboo. Indeed, as memoir has come to be considered a form of its own, its rhetorical devices have grown richer and more varied than ever before.

Feminist Jeanne Perrault asserts that life narratives may be used to help a woman construct both her self and her community. Perrault does not view the "self" as a fixed entity, emphasizing the feminist writer is "both product and producer," there is an ongoing interrelation of self and community.[52] She describes how political/ ideological consciousness takes place at intersections of individual experience in its complexities of race, sexuality, class, ethnicity, thereby contributing to the creation of new communities. From this perspective, women's life narratives not only form the woman who writes, but also the larger feminist movement.

> Each writer [. . .] makes her 'self' the ground of her writing and the scene of her choices, and writing becomes the ground of her (and our) community. The process is recursive: the selves written are transformed in the writing as the communities they change, change them. [53]

Plurality and poly-vocality yield new perspectives, perspectives that create a place to ask ourselves the questions that I imagine Mnemosyne set in motion, questions poet and writer Audre Lourde poses: "What are the words you do not have yet? What do you need to say?"[54]

Henke, psychoanalytic literary critic, first proposed a paradigm for "scripto-therapy," in 1985 by describing the process of writing out and through traumatic experiences in the manner of therapeutic re-enactment.[55] An autobiographer's writing holds the potential of healing the self via the process of reconstructing an earlier story of psychological wounding, offering a way through painful and persistent symptoms. Writing through trauma offers another way of coping with the emotional numbing, dysphoria, and uncontrolled flashbacks common to survivors of deep injuries. It is my contention that as each of us re-collect our stories, we work through our own experiences of fragmentation to create a more manageable narrative. In healing our life's stories, we may effect a shift within the culture which in turn effects individual members of that culture much like the shape of a Möbius strip.

Viewing the aspect of *use* from the mythic perspective of Mnemosyne, one could interpret her intention as that of healing agent, using remembering and re-storying as personal and cultural medicines. For her, the answer to the question of "why this story?" is, at its core, about healing. In birthing the nine Muses, Mnemosyne helps birth various forms of creative expression. In co-creating the arts with her partner Zeus, she engages the process of re-collection and attempts to restore that which has been wounded since the event of her own traumatic birth. Following the associations of her lineage and offspring, one possible use of women's life narratives is that of personal and collective healing

---

Use Exercises:

Answer the questions Audre Lourde poses for yourself: "What are the words you do not have yet? What do you need to say?"

Why do you want to write?

What is it you hope to accomplish?

With whom do you hope to share your stories?

Meeting in the middle

The fourth component of this model is the center, where the aspects of content, form, and use overlap. In my version of a Venn diagram, this area represents an intersection that creates something new. I propose that when considering life narratives, this area becomes an *imaginal field*; here the reader meets the particular woman memoirist as an Other. This space becomes the threshold, a place where one can begin to catch a glimpse of another's reality.

The imaginal field is an initial threshold, a place where intersections merge for both the writer and the reader. Each reading of a book becomes particular; creating new fields of interpretative possibility. The "...text and reader become intertwined, creating new levels of meaning, so that each time we cause the text to yield something upon ingesting it, simultaneously something else is born ..."[56] The text of the memoir or life narrative becomes a place when the reader meets the writer and a new field of understanding is created. It is a place which opens the reader to possibilities, to perspectives, to interrelationships. It is a place where the magic of connection happens.

Recent autobiographies by women demonstrate two kinds of experimental forms; the exploration of daily details and the revelation of fantasies of the writer. The effect of presenting details becomes one of immersion; the imaginal field is entered through the very dailiness of the writer's life. The second, the exploration of the inner world of the woman writer, emphasizes the creative power of the imagination to construct the story. The imaginal field is entered through the "reality" of the writer's imagination and fantasies, a place where the imagination is experienced as its own kind of truth. Patricia Meyer Spacks proposes that women turn inward to the imaginal precisely because of what society prohibits, arguing that women's complex inner lives are the indulgence permitted in place of other privileges. [57]

Elizabeth Spelman notes the importance of imagination as a starting place for shifts in awareness:

> Given [all our] differences, even given oppressive institutions that mangle them, I nonetheless can try,—I must try—to enter imaginatively into the world of others. Imagination isn't enough, but it is necessary. Indeed, it is a crucial starting point: because I have not experienced what the other has, ...

I can't be moved to try to help put an end to her pain or to understand what her pleasures are.[58]

As we think about the imaginal field and Mnemosyne, her lineage comes to the fore. Just as she us offspring of matter and air, the imaginal field is offspring of physical experience and the ephemera of re-collected perceptions. The reader enters a place constructed by the writer, a threshold to experience, and in the reading, a new offspring comes forward. The intersection of the reader's experiences with that of the text creates new perspectives and ways of beginning to understand an "other."

Reflection Exercise:

Have you read a memoir of a person from a different place on the planet or a different culture than your own? Were you offered a threshold? What did you learn? What surprised you? Did you recognize parts of yourself?

Whose stories have you read in which you have found overlapping parts of your own?

Chapter Three:
Take a look in the Mirror

It this section, I would like to think about the Venn diagram and the idea of form, or the shapes our stories take. The metaphor of the mirror is particularly relevant to a discussion of choices of form we make in writing memoir. Humans and mirrors have been paired images throughout history. Pottery images of elegant Corinthians gazing at themselves in small polished disks have been dated as early as the fifth century BCE.[59] Several Greek myths include accounts of mirrors. Medusa's death at the hands of Perseus was accomplished with the aid of highly polished bronze shield which he used as a mirror to deflect her gaze. Narcissus, cursed by a god for his aloofness and emotional insensitivity to other youth and to the nymph Echo, was doomed to fall in love with his own reflected image in a virginal pool of water. The mirror was both beautiful and dangerous. Hephaestus, the god of the forge and metal arts, was imagined as inventor of the mirror. The connection to women and mirrors was developed further in Hephaestus' marriage to Aphrodite and his crafting of beautiful objects for her. The mirror became woven into associations of death/love/betrayal, as well as ordinary vanity. Vase paintings from Archaic Greece show scenes of women with their children and husbands, looking into mirrors and fixing their hair. Women were often portrayed as gazing into hand-held mirrors, though some vase paintings show mirrors hanging on the walls behind the women.[60] Mirrors and women were common topics for painters in Europe from the fourteenth century through the present day. Art critic John Berger writes "The mirror was often used as a symbol of the vanity of women. ... The real function of the mirror was otherwise. It was to make the woman connive in treating herself as, first and foremost, a sight."[61]

Though historically the association between humans and a mirror has underscored vanity, the possibilities of self evaluation have also emerged. In 1954, Norman Rockwell painted an eleven year old girl sitting on a stool contemplating her young self in a mirror with a magazine spread of Jane Russell on her lap. Rockwell's *Girl at the Mirror* is wistful; her face searching the mirror for what her future self might look like. Earlier, in 1946, French painter Balthus presented a young girl on the brink of maturity sitting in front of a tri-fold vanity holding a hand mirror and striking an arched and exaggerated pose. In 1996, California artist Trude McDermott captured a middle aged woman contemplating herself before a large mirror. The image, a photo emulsion piece, was presented in shades of black and white with the exception of the woman's dress, striking in its contrast of deep red. [62] It captures a woman's reflection at mid-life, one capable of exploring the nuances of gray. The image displays how mid-life reflection is a process that begins with curiosity, which is then followed by a frank gaze at what life has brought thus far.

So, how is memoir like a mirror? It begins with reflection, curiosity and a frank gaze, and when it is transcribed, the text reflects back an image. Memoir writing is an attempt to craft an image of a particular self in a particular moment. The writer attempts to capture the essence of this moment of lived experience and present it to the reader for consideration. The image invites and incites reverie. It causes the writer/reader to pause, take the plunge, see what else is swimming below the surface of the re-collected events. Such contemplation makes room for exploring the 'what ifs...' of personal experience, *What if I had not met X? What if I had not moved to Y? What if I had said Z?* Reverie activates the imagination and the story one sets out to tell is deepened and re-figured in the process.

In a foreword to Robert Romanyshn's *Mirror and Metaphor,* David Miller notes that "...reflection ... does not tell what things are, but gives an image of what they are like. ...It has to do with making metaphors. Reflection is the soul musing about matters."[63] This is relevant to the memoirist. Just as a mirror reflection begins with a frank gaze, memoir begins with reflection about oneself in the present moment. The text takes its form through a selection of metaphors. We look in a mirror and attempt to "see" our self, to note the image our self presents at that moment. When we craft a text, we also attempt to "see" an image of a self we are attempting to give form to in words. Romanyshyn goes on to describe how the mirror functions as an instrument of projection, "I never look into the mirror as much as I look through it or beyond it .... the mirror ... disappears to become a medium or a pivot or an axis through which the reflected and reflection communicate."[64] Memoir also functions in this manner; the text becomes a medium through which memories and the images they evoke begin to speak. For Romanyshyn the image is not a mere double of the person, but rather a "figure in a story."[65] As the writer of memoir is aware, choices of content and form give representations of experiences, not the experience itself. Memoir creates a snapshot, or a video segment, of a particular self at a particular time in a particular place, and the memoirist herself becomes a figure in a story told at that particular moment.

Like the mirror, memoir implicates and questions notions of the self. Who is writing the story? Is the author conscious of being the participant/protagonist, the witness/observer, the reflective consciousness in her own story? Is the author conscious of her gendered self, that her presentation is necessarily a gendered performance of the self? Is the author aware of her self through the lens of culture and social class? Memoir, like the mirror, sets one questioning who is really there in the image which looks back at us.

Memoir, like a mirror, frames experience. It necessarily chooses what to include, what to leave out in the interests shaping the text. Memoir necessarily selects one aspect, one facet of a life to explore. The investigation is about this one aspect, and presenting it with as much clarity as possible. Like a mirror, memoir still reflects even in fragments; from a single episode a whole life unfolds, much like a dream image or a hologram.

When one first begins writing memoir, the initial task is to learn to sit still and to craft pictures with words, which describe events, people, and places of one's life through the act of simple reflection. One forces oneself to look in the mirror and to call up the stories that live there. In the process, the author not only records experiences, but also offers a gift to her readers through the meaning she makes of her reflections. Beginning to write causes one to realize that the only stories one can tell are one's own. We may not have stories to pass down from the mouths of our foremothers or forefathers, but we can use our own words to tell our own stories. In this process, we can trust that the unspoken stories of the ancestor-line will emerge in the background, much as Lillian Hellman's describes an artist's *pentimento*:

> Old paint on canvas, as it ages, sometimes becomes transparent. When that happens it is possible, in some pictures, to see the original lines: a tree will show through a woman's dress, a child makes way for a dog, a large boat is no longer on an open sea. That is called *pentimento* because the painter "repented," changed his mind. Perhaps it would be as to say that the old conception, replaced by a later choice, is a way of seeing and then seeing again.[66]

Of course, simple reflection is not so simple after all. When we stop to ponder the various mirrors given to us by our culture and subcultures, we realize these particular mirrors may be cracked or warped. Through the act of simple self-reflection one confronts basic incongruities and begins to consider the complexities of life experience. Simple reflection offers an overview for the content of the material to be worked in a piece of memoir. As with the pool of Narcissus, the story being contemplated sends one into reverie, a place where other insights swim just under the surface, a place of transitory awareness, a place of association and dream-like images. Doing the work of memoir in this manner, this reflecting in a 'down and in' posture, is much like the tradition of sacred cup divination common to antiquity. The re-collection of memories is not about seeing something meaningful in a particular event, but pondering the event and letting what's meaningful surface.

Kinds of mirrors: Reflections, Distortions, Forms

David Miller observes that art history provides a differentiated picture of the technology of the development of the mirror and identifies five types of mirrors and the qualities of reflection and distortion offered by each.[67] Each of these different kinds of mirrored surfaces provides a perspective, a way of viewing which corresponds to choices of form used in creating memoir.

The first mirrors were likely pools of water. The characteristics of such a surface suggest a kind of depth, awareness of ripples, of darker tones. In a watery mirror, one is aware of change in the image reflected. The surface may ripple, the current may shift, some creature may swim up from the depths and break up the image, or set it in motion. The tone is somber, aware of the transitory nature of the image reflected. Such surfaces call up associations to Narcissus and Shakespeare's Ophelia. Both of these images underscore the relationship of death with watery mirrors and with the unconscious. Miller suggests that the mirror of water suggests a depth, a way to deepen imaginative reflection.

In making analogy to a form for memoir, a water mirror presents story as reverie and association. Using this kind of mirror means writing with a "down and in" kind of posture, that suggests a way of examining an event more deeply than simply staying with the literal moment. This kind of mirror presents memoir as a mode of deep reflection, a mode that ponders, then watches what swims to the surface. It requires stillness and a willingness to look below the shimmering surface into the depths and to let images arise. Bachelard notes that water as a mirror provides the opportunity for open imagination; it invites one to stretch out arms and thrust one's own hands down and into one's own image.[68] The form follows associations, takes its time, and attempts to portray the complexity of emotional and psychological experience.

A recent example of such a work is Terry Tempest William's *Leap* in which she associates her spiritual and vocational life to a painting, Bosch's *Garden of Delights*, that hung over her bed at her Mormon grandmother's house. As she takes her time with each image within the painting, she looks into the depths of her life and describes the moments which came to shape her views on religion and the environment. The book follows each segment of the triptych: Paradise, Hell, and the Garden of Earthly Delights. Each segment of the memoir traces the themes presented in the landscape of the painting and associates each with her experiences as a child and as a young adult, articulating moments of clarity which formed her sense of self and her ongoing spiritual evolution. It is a book written with a long, deep look, a gaze that captures the myriad of creatures which swim below the surface and bears witness to the boundless realm of imagination.

Concave metal mirrors became more common as metallurgy developed during the European Copper, Bronze and Iron Ages (ca. 4000 B.C.E. to 100 B.C.E.).[69] In such reflective surfaces, the image is concentrated and larger than life. Proportions change, and the focus changes with the focal length. Such mirrors also present the image as upside down, lending intentional distortion as well as the possibility of a divine/transpersonal perspective to the idea of mirroring. [70] An example of such a mirror is the "scrying cup," like the one described in the story of Joseph in Genesis. The "scryer" purports to look in the cup and divine important events. A person looks into the shiny surface until a trance state is attained, external vision clouded, preparing the scryer for possible visions. Such a concave surface serves to diffuse normal sight, which is further blurred by the burnished face of the metal. Visions are possible when literal sight is overcome.[71]

Another example of a concave mirror in the present day is the astronomical lens. The concave surface is also useful for distant images, to enable us to see things beyond the scope of human vision. In 1773, William Herschel, an expatriate German musician living in England began crafting concave metallic mirrors that he would turn to the skies. Such mirrors became "...sacred eyes, peering ever farther into the mysteries of God's universe."[72] From the scryer's cup to the telescope, the concave mirror evokes a sense of connection with that which is beyond daily experience, beyond literal vision.

Texts that are analogous to the concave mirror record moments of "revelation," spiritual apology, descriptions of mystical religious experiences like those of Hildegard of Bingen, or contemporary poet and memoirist Kathleen Norris. The form here attempts to convey moments of clarity, of seeing beyond oneself and making relationship to the transcendent. Kathleen Norris's *Dakota: A Spiritual Geography* is a memoir shaped by her exploration of landscape and her own evolving spirituality. She brings together weather reports, poetry, American history, family vignettes, and personal experiences. In each of these segments, she communicates a sense of discovery of the sacred in everyday life, a sense of finding a relationship to the mysteries of human existence. The concave mirror is a good metaphor for memoirs that recognize, in the words of Lynda Sexson, "[that] Peculiar moments in ordinary lives, saturated by metaphor or personal symbol making, are the stuff of religion." [73] The concave mirror yields a form that names the "ordinarily sacred" moments of a life, which finds the "...sacred within the secular, or the divine in the ordinary." [74]

The convex glass mirror came into existence around 100 B.C.E. as Syrian craftsmen experimented with dipping a long hollow tube in a vat of molten glass and then blowing through the tube. The result was the invention of hollowware that was eventually also crafted into small convex pocket mirrors. Glass was blown into spheres, and hot lead then poured inside as a coating. The spheres were then carefully broken and cut into small mirrors. These became very popular throughout the Roman Empire; they were used in homes and have been found in grave sites all over the area. Production of such mirrors fell into decline with the fall of Rome, and didn't reappear in most of Europe until the twelfth century.[75]

The reflective image in a convex mirror, as in the concave mirror, presents a distortion. The image in the center is enlarged along with an increased capacity to show peripheral images. The world can appear in miniature with this type of mirror, because lines are straighter and edges sharper. Miller says "...the principal function of a convex mirror is to miniaturize and clarify, in short, to focus and give order to what the mirror can take from a broad periphery." [76] Paradoxically, these distortions can also bring order, clarity and intensity.

A text working with this kind of mirror will take its form by getting the details in sharp focus, in the way of letters or diaries, and journal-style writing. Such forms are unapologetic; they present the writer as the central protagonist of her story. Her image is central and images of relationships and details of her life are presented as part of the broad periphery of her life. This mirror is in the tradition of Rousseau's *Confessions* and more recently, Kate Millett's *Flying*. Using this form entails the inclusion of as many details as the writer can recall; it focuses on moments of experience and displays a conviction of the importance of self expression. Another such example is Brenda Ueland's *Me:A Memoir.* She wrote in 1938 from the perspective of a mid-western city woman. A daughter of Norwegian immigrants born in 1891, in Minneapolis, Minnesota, she was privileged to attend Barnard College at the turn of the century and worked as a free-lance journalist. She frequented Greenwich Village and spent time with Jack Reed, Emma Goldman, and Edith Lewis. She was married and divorced by the time she was in her forties, and would marry again twice more. Her memoir gives a sharp sense of what it must have been like to be a woman who was educated, a rule breaker, and always interested in the events of her time in an American city before World War II. Her form is epistolary; she is frank about her experiences and just as frank about the ones she chooses not to share. She addresses her readers directly, keeping the language conversational. The resulting structure of her book is very much a look into the convex mirror; the reader has a particular appreciation for the woman Brenda Ueland and for the broad periphery of the particular historical world in which she lived.

The plate glass mirror first came into production around 1507 in Venice. It was made possible by improvements in the manufacture of larger and larger sheets of blown glass as well as by the discovery of techniques of applying silver backing. Clarity continued to improve as Venetians approximated the processes of silvering with the combination of tin and mercury solutions. It would be almost two more centuries before glass could be cast in panes rather than cut from blown spheres. The French manufacturers from Saint-Gobain perfected production of large cast mirrors, increasing both the size and uniform thickness of the glass. The reflection of this kind of mirror offers a clear and distinct representation, as well as the possibility of multiple perspectives on the image in reflection.

The disadvantages of the plate mirror are that it flattens and reflects only what is placed directly before it. It necessarily leaves objects beyond its frame out of the reflection, and the effect of framing the image then causes an interpretation of what is presented.

David Miller describes how the effect of the plate mirror changes the perception of the image by

> ...collapsing moisture's depth, concave breadth, and convex intensity into the merely real, as opposed to the really real. ... Flat mirrors may be useful for admiration, but scrying becomes problematic, since the flat mirror seduces the imaginal prophetic vision outward into the literalism of external knowing.[77]

The flat glass mirror takes away the sense of magic, of the possibilities of connection with realities beyond literal matter. It tends toward a social realism, rather than a more romantic view of the world.

A memoir which uses this kind of mirror will tell the story in as straightforward a manner as possible. The form will concentrate on the present moment, a frank gaze at what is and consideration of the events which have led up to this moment. It will demonstrate a capacity for multiple viewpoints, as there may be other figures in the same frame who will necessarily have unique perspectives on the images being reflected.

Carolyn Kay Steedman's *Landscape for a Good Woman* is an example of using a plate glass mirror kind of text. She lines up the story of her own childhood alongside the story of her mother's working class life, and in the process crafts a discussion of aspects of women's lives which are not easy or pleasant to contemplate: poverty, illegitimacy, disappointment, envy, and hopelessness. She looks into the mirror and describes what she sees: a daughter of a working class English woman who grew up without a father. Her way of "telling it straight" involves recognition of multiple vantage points from which a woman's identity emerges. She challenges two prominent ways of reading/representing identity; that of Marxist class critique and psychoanalysis. Neither are adequate to the task of describing her mother's life or her own. Steedman maintains that a woman's identity is always multi-textual, embedded in other women's stories, influenced by competing interpretations. Her book is one example of memoir written from the perspective of a flat glass mirror, a mirror that reflects unflinchingly that which is placed before it and reflects not only the woman who writes, but the women who live in her face and her bones, the women who came before her.

Another example of this kind of mirror text form is Patricia Hampl's *A Romantic Education.* She chooses her frame, the exploration of her ancestral lineage from Bohemia in what is now the Czech Republic. Her recollections begin with her grandmother's photo album of '*Zlata Praha*'and proceed with a collection of episodes that reflect the process by which she comes to make meaning out of her ethnic heritage, culminating in Hampl's first visit to Prague in 1975 during the Cold War. Her writing also acknowledges the multiple perspectives of social identity, of the complexities involved in coming to terms with what being a contemporary American woman means, particularly when the same mirror reflects a contemporary Czech woman from Prague by her side. This memoir, shaped by the plate glass mirror, is aware of its generational limitations, as well as its ability to present images in sharp relief, and to recognize the many angles of perspective which are possible within a given frame.

The final mirror that Miller identifies is the broken mirror, as represented by Picasso in his 1932 painting "The Girl Before the Mirror." In this cubist portrayal, the idea of the mirror as it had been previously portrayed is broken; the idea of literal verisimilitude is now in pieces. A reflection becomes much more complicated. Instead of a single undifferentiated image, there are now "...a plurality of reflections, [and] the rich multifaceted sparkle of Being."[78] Picasso's image declares reflection is not simple, uniform, or predictable. Indeed the shattered mirror suggests multiple perspectives, the possibility of interiority, and the gaze as a potentially mutual endeavor between the woman and her reflection.

Writing with this kind of mirror celebrates fragments, discontinuous narrative, and non-chronological presentations. Such a mirror presents episodic recollections and is willing to imagine what lives in the mirror as its own entity. A broken mirror acknowledges the possibility that a part can summon the whole, that a single episode can metonymously conjure a whole life. The broken mirror doesn't mind mixing aspects of many genres: dialogue, personal vignettes, imaginal scenes, historical contexts, social-political commentary, and poetry are all potential pieces in the collage memoir constructs.

Maxine Hong Kingston's memoir, *The Woman Warrior: Memoirs of a Girlhood Among the Ghosts,* is an example of reflection via a broken mirror. She re-collects herself through a variety of forms–personal vignettes of her childhood, fictions she makes for herself, and fantasies which celebrate magical realism. Her interest is in the imaginal possibilities, in the conviction that the inner life of the imagination is also real, that the image in the mirror really *is* looking back and has something to say. The book describes her experience of being raised in America by her Chinese immigrant mother, of the clashes between what being a woman meant in China and in the United States in the 1950s. She refracts the difficulties of speaking up, of finding her voice, of writing, and creating new stories for herself.

Kingston retells a story fragment about an aunt who killed herself upon the birth of an illegitimate child, holding the piece up and turning it this way and that, exploring the possibilities of what might have happened and seeing herself mirrored in the same story. Her imaginal crafting of the myth of Fa Mu Lan as part of her own history is set next to her recollection of her childhood in San Francisco. Such positioning of stories is much like Picasso's broken mirror: each piece presents a unique reflection and each adds depth and color to the representation of this particular woman's life. Hong Kingston is aware that the edges of the pieces are sharp, words can cut, wield power, create change. Hers is a memoir aware of the need to claim the power of the broken mirror, to claim its capacity to reflect personal and collective histories, to celebrate the dance of possibilities that lie behind, within, and before us.

Alice Walker's *The Way Forward is with a Broken Heart* is another example of a memoir written from a broken mirror like perspective. Like Hong Kingston, she is not adverse to crafting an imaginal memoir, one that weaves together the facts and fantasies of her life. She begins in the Preface acknowledging the reality of her ten year marriage to a man who was foreign to her; he was Jewish and from New York, she was African American and Southern. The book is the story of their inter-racial marriage at the time of the civil rights movement in the United States. The first chapter begins with a letter to her young husband, and proceeds with a set of stories which she describes as "mostly fiction" in the service of best representing her experience of those ten years, and how they came to shape her life's work as a feminist and writer. The stories weave first person and third person narratives, and the epilogue concludes with another address to her former husband, written in the present. This memoir is another example of how a broken mirror holds the potential for new ways of reflecting the self, ways which value the worth and dignity present in the fragments we cherish as memories.

In contemplating these five kinds of mirrors, one can explore the ways in which mirrors offer perspective and present various inflections of images. Each mirror finds correspondence in various forms of text, offering unique modes for relating and creating a memoir. Writing memoir is a process of reflecting, one which can become vertiginous. As one looks in the mirror to call up the stories, one is also aware of crafting another mirror with the construction of a text. The conscious choice of a mirror becomes a choice of form and can shift points of access and recognition within the text. The story can be accented differently with the choice of mirror; slow in the mode of reverie, connected to the sacred in ordinary moments, focused on the daily details of personal experience, unflinching in its presentation of what stands before it, and aware of the evocative power of fragments.

Another possible "mirror mode" for construction of memoir is that of the kaleidoscope, a device that functions by way of internal mirrors placed in relationship to one another. The images viewed from a kaleidoscope are both beautiful and intriguing, resulting from investigations into the nature of light and reflection. Working with Ptolemy's discovery of the patterns of repeated and symmetrical forms that appear when multiple mirrors are placed in relationship to one another, the kaleidoscope's inventor was intent at first on creating instruments which could make visual displays that paralleled the production of harmonics in music. The kaleidoscope was invented by David Brewster in 1819. He decided to add both movement and color to his experiments, resulting in the phenomenon of myriad optical designs.

Brewster chose the name based on three Greek words: *kalos* beautiful + *eidos* form + *skopeo* I see; suggesting a name meaning "a viewer of beautiful forms." The construction of the scope is relatively simple. Two inclined mirrors form an open prism along the axis of a tube, which has a peep hole on one end. The other end is closed by a cell of two glass plates between which some small colored objects are placed. When the tube is held to the light, the colored objects are reflected in both mirrors and the two series of reflections, both returning to themselves, create regular polygonal patterns. Another modification by Brewster was the 'teleidoscope'. In this variation, the cell with the colored pieces is replaced by a convex mirror through which everyday objects can be viewed. The result is seeing the objects of daily life in miniature, as well as seeing them multiplied in symmetrically arranged polygons which fill the field of vision.[79] Such a vision yields a continuous flow of movement, one further exaggerated by the distance from the object. Wolfgang Zucker describes it thus:

> As the viewer changes the distance to the object, the ornament acquires a most intriguing dynamic, centrifugal and centripetal at the same time. With every slight shift of the tube, new elements unfold themselves out of the center and radiate toward the periphery. These spread out over the whole field, while they simultaneously are succeeded by new forms and colors, coming out of the inexhaustible point of origin, where the ornamental pattern is both simultaneously born and annihilated. [80]

There is much metaphorical resonance in this image for the memoirist. It leads one to muse on the components chosen to do the viewing, and the realization that the choice of components, from containers to lenses, from mirrors to rings, influences what will be seen and how it will be viewed. Each viewpoint provides unique information and perspective on what is being considered. Each aspect provides *a* perspective, a *partial* view. The views from the kaleidoscope are analogous to the different kinds of mirrors previously mentioned. Different mirrors and mirroring systems create different kinds of perspectives.

The memoirist takes the fragments of memory, drops them in the object chamber of the kaleidoscope and views them from a variety of angles. Perspective shifts as time passes. Story, particularly personal narrative, becomes the "ornament" which shifts. Shaping particular events changes as life moves through and around the story teller. At different times, some constructions will emphasize relationships, others emotional states, others particular places; all tellings become kaleidoscopic variations with their own unique pattern. Each memoirist will have a unique collection of containers, mirrors, and rings which will inform her particular interpretation of life experiences. While each woman's life provides her with unique content for consideration, it is up to each woman writer to place it in her own containers, constructed from those vantage points which she has found useful, and begin the dance of mirrors, the (de) construction of meaning which it calls forth.

The literary term, *mise en abyme,* is also related to the theme of multiple viewpoints with mirroring and memoir. Lucien Dallenbach offers a fine multivalent analysis of the term, drawing attention to the fact that the "mirror in the text" has multiple meanings: simple duplication, infinite duplication, and aporetic duplication[81] In simple duplication, there is simple reflection and reference to basic metaphor. In the case of infinite duplication, there is a possibility of an infinite regression to no-thing-ness, much like a piece of art by M.C. Escher. This is the realm of metonymy, a place where a thing can be called up by naming one of its attributes. This kind of duplication becomes a place where ultimate meaning is deferred, a place which is gappy and full of paradoxes. This kind of perspective can be likened to a broken mirror in which the pieces reflect their own unique and sparkling perspective, yielding a beautiful kaleidoscopic view.[82]

In J. Hillis Miller's *Ariadne's Thread,* aporia is described as an "...impasse, the absence, in a sequential argument, of a way out of or a way beyond." [83] The idea of aporia underscores the impossibility of an original form with a singular interpretation and emphasizes each reflection as new and generative.

Consideration of such patterns allows for the appreciation of both the complexity and simplicity present in the act of reflection. It also allows the memoirist to contemplate the way each act of reflection is new and unpredictable, influenced by myriad life experiences. Each minute of life adds further complexities and possibilities to the reflected episode, the stories we choose to tell can never be told the same way twice. As one begins the process of creating memoir, other mirrors may open in the center of our reflections: the mirror of oneself as a child with the reflection of one's own injuries, as well as the reflections of injured parents and ancestors who stand just behind. Memoir, however, can serve as witness to these experiences by conveying the emotional tone of peering into such a long line of mirrors. Mirrors of mothers who could not celebrate what had not been celebrated for them or for their mothers, even mirrors of mothers who could not speak up for their daughters because they could not speak up for themselves. It is important for a writer of memoir to offer opportunities to peer down such corridors and pause. We not only have a physical lineage, but emotional, spiritual, and imaginal ones as well. It is good to remember where we have come from. The dark stories and the stories that are present by their very absence, are stories that can offer maps which are useful as we make our own paths through life.

Ultimately, it does not really matter if the mirror is broken, if the story is told in fragments. The very cracks in the mirror, in the story we think we are telling, are what give our re-collections their unique expression. As Mieke Bal says, the cracks in the mirror leave us "... with a fragmentation that we can live with. Only within these cracks, and if we are mindful of them, can a conversation take place."[84] Shards of memories form a kind of mirror play, a back-and-forth motion in which everything in the world reflects everything else. In the words of David Miller, "...mirrors mirroring mirrors, up and down, in and out. And everything is a mirror when reflected upon, for in the reflections the world twinkles back at us."[85]

The *simulacrum* is another important concept for the memoirist contemplating which kind of mirror to use, which kind of form to choose. The literal definition of the word means "an image or representation," but critic Gilles Deleuze describes the term as an affirmation of simple, present tense experience. He traces the duality of idea and image to Plato, distinguishing between the *copy*, an image closely resembling the archetypal original, and the *simulacrum*, an image unconcerned with exact likeness to the original. As a memoirist, I find this viewpoint helpful. It speaks to the nature of memory itself. Trying to capture a past event on paper just as it occurred is an impossible task. One can only re-collect an assemblage of images and feeling tones. The memoirist creates a telling of events, crafting a fragment of a mirror. Simulacrum can offer surprises because it can be viewed not as a degraded copy, but as something with its own kind of positive power.[86] The recollection of these elements is a similacrum of those moments being called back. One can never go back to a particular moment and experience the circumstances in exactly the same manner. Instead of being overly critical of one's inability to "get it right," of being able to portray the poignancy of events, the memoirist is able to relax into the dance of mirrors. From this perspective, each piece of writing, with its attempts to peel back layers of experience, becomes an expression of the events. If details are recalled differently from one telling to the next, they become valuable nuances of the story, rather than an admission of imperfect story telling skills. Memoir, much like the process of analysis, becomes a process of retelling a life in both the past, present, and possible future. As the memoirist creates her particular story, she is met by the reader and in being read/heard, both are changed.

The questions for a woman memoirist become: which mirror to use? Which mirror/kind of form am I hungry for? Can I identify the mirror I am using? Is it being used consciously or unconsciously? Can I see my own distortions? Am I aware that my choice of mirror will influence what will be storied? Can the mirror choose me and my story?

Mirror exercises:

Do you have any memories of specific mirrors as you were growing up? Did you ever break a mirror? What happened?

Are there particular surfaces that set you into reverie? What are they?

What are your personal experiences with each of these kinds of mirrors...is one more interesting to you that the others? Why?

Chapter Four
The Muses: Multiplicity of Forms

Because I imagine Mnemosyne standing behind the writer of memoir, I find much in her story which is helpful in considering the *forms* we can choose when we write memoir. Because she is a Titan daughter of the Earth Herself, it is in her nature to produce *embodied* forms of expression. Her gifts are being able to take memories from what Shakespeare's King Theseus called the "airy nothing" in *Midsummer Night's Dream*—the stuff of her Father Sky, and ground them in word, voice, poem, story, song, dance, ritual, and study. The memoirist stands in Mnemosyne's lineage as she re-collects particular events and constructs a text which will bring these wisps and fragments of sensory impressions into material form.

The Greeks understood Mnemosyne's capacity for multiple forms by virtue of her daughters, the Muses. There is evidence in Pausinias to earlier Greek texts of two generations of Muses; the first comprised of just three feminine characters, *Melete*- Preparation, *Mneme*- Memory, and *Aiode*- Song, but by the time of Hesiod, a second generation of nine Muses are present.[87] In Hesiod's *Theogony,* the Muses are described as the offspring of a divine love between the Titan Mnemosyne, whose maternal proclivities toward embodiment were further amplified by the ordering principles of their father, Zeus. Each Muse was ascribed a particular form of expression; they were known to the Greeks as: Euterpe, Terpsichore, Calliope, Clio, Melpomene, Urania, Thalia, Polyhymnia, and Erato. Gail Thomas describes the Muses as figures who "...educate our soul: they teach us to be able to hold *forms* in the soul, forms that guide us making music, in moving, in speaking, in writing, in grieving, in worshiping, in playing, in singing, and in loving."[88] While Thomas is particularly interested in how the Muses are present in contemporary culture, and especially in the ways they inform the making of cities, I am interested in their influence on *form* for writers of memoir. Viewed from Mnemosyne's vantage point, women's memoir can, of course, take multi-forms; she gave birth to nine Muses, nine vantage points, each with her own unique perspective, her own creative mode. Mnemosyne as mother of the Muses celebrates the multiplicity of ways memory can be expressed.

Angeles Arrien, anthropologist and author, explores the nine Muses and the various forms each inflects as guide for personal creativity. She goes on to explain that while each Muse has her own realm, each is also "capable of suggesting the range of all the disciplines taken together. Each of the Muses represents a path to creativity and has her own distinct role or function in leading us further into our creative lives..."[89] This aspect of the Muses is related to another characteristic of Mnemosyne: her ability to call up a whole through a part. Memories evoked by the scent of bread baking can call up an entire scene from one's childhood, and from that one scene, a whole life, and from that life, a family, from that family, a culture. Circles then become nested in circles. Memoir can begin with the musing on sensory fragments, and after reflection, manifest in myriad ways. Text can be historical under the musing of Clio, sorrowful by way of Melpomene, reverent under Polyhymnia, comic by Thalia, musical under the influence of Euterpe, heroic by Calliope, full of desire and remembrances of love by way of Erato, kinesthetic and embodied with Terpsichore, and metaphysical and other worldly with the soft eyes of Urania. Each Muse evokes a particular form, one which can both call a story forth and give it shape.

Not all art forms practiced in Greek culture were given a presiding Muse. Weaving, crafting of pottery and metals, painting and sculpture were left out of the specific realms of the Muses, though some of these production arts were associated with other Greek divinities. Scholar Barbara Hort suggests that the Greeks perceived a more mysterious relationship between the 'ephemeral' arts and the Muses:

It is important to remember that there were no methods in ancient Greece for recording sound and movement, including spoken language, song, and dance. This means that the Muses presided over art forms that were necessarily ephemeral, largely manifested and recorded only within the bodies of the artists and their audiences. Once those bodies died, most of those Muse-inspired arts were doomed to die along with them. Then as today, once a stone is sculpted there is a sculpture, but once a song is sung, there is silence.[90]

The arts which manifested through the voice, music, words, and movement were experienced as performance events which could not be captured for repeated enjoyment. Because of their unique 'in the moment' qualities, such artistic expressions were highly valued and seen as mystical in nature.

Mnemosyne's Touch: Multiplicity of Forms Exercises in Perspective shifts

a) Recall a pivotal moment, a time when something important happened, a time after which you knew things would never be quite the same again. Now write it in third person, or as "once upon a time...", or from the first person perspective of another person or object involved in the story

b) Recall an early memory: write it from the vantage point of scent and texture; now write it from sight and sound...now write it from taste

c) Recall your first pet; from your point of view, then the pet's point of view

d) Recall your favorite food as a child; from your point of view,

then the point of view of the one who prepared the food or the venue who served it...

Clio

Each Muse offers the writer of memoir a different way into telling her stories, each offering a different avenue for shaping recollections. At first glance it would seem Clio, the daughter designated to inspire history, would be the primary figure for those attempting to make a record of a life. Her name comes from the Greek verb *klein, to tell* and *to celebrate.* Clio evokes telling and celebrating. Eileen Gregory describes her as one who tells a story simply, not for the sake of telling a story but of telling it to set the record straight, to lay out the facts. [91] It is through her impulse that one desires to give an account of the events of one's life. Gregory points out that

> History is a mode of understanding, having to do with a clear-sighted view of the constants of human nature, thus of the repetitive character of human events as political and natural situations compelling decisions that test human judgment and will in all its fallibility. The testimony, the simple telling, of what happened in a moment of great significance is pointed to the future, is oriented to the timeless in some way. [92]

Clio's relationship to memoir understands the importance of recounting the story of one's life, of sifting through the details in order to make a record of the events with a more dispassionate eye. Her delight is in the investigation of connections, of finding out how things are related in ways not seen before. She is the one who helps the memoirist contextualize her life story, offering a way of seeing the personal within the framework of larger social and cultural events of the time. She is the muse who would prefer the plate glass mirror, with its unflinching reflection of what is placed before it and its ability to reflect multiple figures within the same frame. Helen Buss explains memoir and Clio's influence thus:

> ...(memoir) is a form in which one can not rely on the facts of official history, yet it is a form in which one can not dispense with historical narrative. .... Most important, the memoir is a form in which history must come into concourse with

literature in order to make a self, a life, and to locate that living self in a history, and era, a relational and communal identity. [93]

One such contemporary example of a memoir written under Clio's influence is *What Would My Mother Say: A Tribal Girl of Africa Comes of Age in America.* It is written by Dympna Ugwu-Oju, a Nigerian born woman raised in a traditional Ibo culture, who lives through the turmoil of civil war, and comes to live in the United States. Her story unfolds after the birth of her third child as she and her husband decide to make the United States, not Nigeria, their permanent home. Her story recounts the complexity of being a woman born in a culture where girls are customarily given in arranged marriages, bride prices are paid, and a wife is not permitted to meet her husband's eyes. Because Dympna is a good student, she is given the opportunity to study in the United States where she earns degrees from both Briarcliff College and Syracuse University. Despite the shifts in her perspectives, she returns to Nigeria and decides to go through with a traditional arranged marriage. Despite her adherence to some of the traditional Ibo gender boundaries, she becomes the first woman to hold a professorial position in mass communications in Nigeria. Her memoir portrays the multiple conflicts of a contemporary woman struggling to come to terms with clashing cultures, the roles of women, raising children, and the legacy of her mother-line. Ugwu-Oju is trained as a journalist and presents a straight forward narrative which situates her own story in relation to the larger historical and cultural forces of her time. It is a frank look in a plate glass mirror, one which captures the multiplicity of relationships in one woman's reflection. Ugwu-Oju's story can be imagined as a narrative inspired by Clio, the muse who calls for tracing the line from one culture to another, each formative relationship, each educational and vocational achievement.

Clio "History, events as they occurred"

a) Create a personal history list:

Begin with your birth and continue by creating a list of all your life's important events and relationships. You may have hundreds of items. This can be a useful aid as it may help you to focus on things that deserve the most attention. It also primes the pump of memory: the more you write, the more you'll remember. Your list will continue to grow, as the list gets longer, organize it chronologically.

b) Now choose ten items that you feel were the most formative.

Select one and write the event as succinctly as you can.

Re-write it as a narrative, use 'softer eyes'.

c) Look through a scrapbook... your photo collection or a high school year book... select an image of yourself and write a story of that day. Let one picture catch your eye or allow a succession of images provide insight into someone's development or decline. Let these images inspire you to write –about the time, incidents, or emotions the photographs evoke. You may notice a pattern in the photos you have saved. What images have you chosen to keep? Notice the changes wrought by age and fashion. What do these photos say about the people who shot them? What do they say about the times when they were taken? Pay attention to what is not in the picture as well as what sits in the periphery. If you are writing about another time and place, you will find old picture books a valuable resource. Look carefully at the hairstyles, the clothing, the props.

d) Try looking through the daily newspaper; the want ads, the obituaries, the business section, the sports or local events. Notice which articles grab your attention, what they remind you of. You may find a bit of personal history gets jogged, write it down!

e) Is there someone form your past that you would like to write a letter? A friend? A teacher? A former spouse? Try writing to them and say what you were never able to tell this person. Share some of the insights you've gained since your last communication. You need not mail this letter—simply voice your thoughts and feelings on paper.

f) Create a background file on one of the important people in your life. Try Ira Progoff's Stepping Stones technique— imagine the twelve most significant events in a relative's life starting with birth and ending with the present moment. ...try to imagine his/her history, the daily details of their life. How many children, if any, did this person have? Where did he/she work? Was there a major crisis in this person's life? Look for clues in your subject's dress, location, and demeanor. Develop several different scenarios, how might this particular story have unfolded? You can interpret character to mean place, invention, or institution. Imagine the people who occupied a house over several generations. Picture the dramas that occurred in various rooms. What was the neighborhood like when the house was first built?

Calliope

Calliope was described by Hesiod as the daughter who "holds the highest position" among the Muses. Her area of inspiration is that of epic poetry and the art of the spoken word. Angeles Arrien describes her as one of the most eloquent of her sisters due to "...her remarkable ability to synthesize all known forms of poetry, song, and music into the organization of dramatic presentations known as epic poetry. Epic poems often tell the story of cultural values and beginnings of a journey— of a country, a race or a hero." [94] Her name comes from the Greek *kalliope,* meaning "fine strong voice." Dona Gower points out that Calliope's intention is not only to give shape to the stories of ancient heroes, but also to the stories of those who live in the present. "The present hero must also learn to sing his own story, to make meaning through Calliope's gift of eloquent speech, so that his life becomes a poem for himself as well as for others."[95] This is the Muse who inspires the memoirist to create a "personal mythology," a way of living and telling one's life story with a mythic lens. Psychologist June Singer describes mythic perspective, Calliope's lens, like this:

> To live mythically means to become aware of your personal and collective origins. In the process of learning to do this, you will discover, or affirm, that you are not an isolated, independent being, but the end product of the millennia of acculturation and maturation of the human race. Personal mythology is but the flower on the bush: the family myth is the branch, society's conventions form the stem, and the root is the human condition. Personal myths structure our awareness and point us in the direction that becomes our path.[96]

Calliope provides a way of story telling imbued with poetic sensibility. That poetic sensibility manifests in structural devices such as repetition, pause, and familiar phrases so that the audience and performer can integrate the major elements being presented. The memoirist also relies on such structural devices, attempting to recreate events within the rhythm of language and syntax. Under Calliope's influence, a fluid quality to the prose invites reverie. A recent memoir by Barbara Robinette Moss, *Change Me Into Zeus's Daughter*, offers an example of Calliope's influence. A haunting story about growing up poor in the South, Moss undertakes the recitation of her family's survival in the rural hills of Alabama in the early 1960s. Her father was a wild alcoholic who disappeared for long periods, leaving his brood of seven, and later nine, children and his wife to fend for themselves. She begins her story with a chapter titled, "Near the Center of the Earth."

> Mother spooned the poisoned corn and beans into her mouth, ravenously, eyes closed, hands shaking. We, her seven children, sat around the table watching her for signs of death, our eyes leaving her only long enough to glance at the clock

to see how far the hands had moved. Would she turn blue, like my oldest sister Alice said? Alice sat hunched next to me in the same white kitchen chair, our identical homemade cotton dresses blending into one. She shoved my shoulder with hers as if I were disturbing her concentration and stared not blinking at Mother. Each time Mother hesitated, spoon in midair, Alice's face clouded and she pushed against my shoulder.

"She's dying," Alice whispered, covering her mouth so Mother could not hear. "I told you she was gonna die."

I ignored her and watched Mother. I wanted to feel the kernels of sweet yellow corn slide against my teeth. I didn't care if they were poisoned. I was so hungry my head throbbed. ....[97]

Moss grows up in the grip of malnutrition which causes facial deformity, what she comes to describe as her "twisted mummy face." She expresses an early fascination with art and literature which coincides with her desire to transform herself through education and eventually, corrective surgery. In her Acknowledgements she says her intention in writing this story was "...to go back in time—to heal old wounds and reclaim my family." She writes her own heroic transformation and bears witness to the beauty in herself and others who are woven in her family tapestry. Calliope's influence bears witness to moments of profound courage and bravery.

Calliope is the Muse who couples with a river god and bears Orpheus, the famed Thracian singer who charmed all living things with his beautiful voice and lyre playing. In this genealogical association, Mnemosyne and her daughters are linked with water. Water has long been associated with emotion life, subjectivity and with depth of feeling. For the Greeks, the ephemeral arts had a special relationship with the qualities of water. The birth place of the Muses was Mt. Helicon in Greece, a terrain which evokes associations of streams, rivers, springs and water moving and sounding over rocks and in creek beds. Barbara Hort observes that Muse forms are water-like; they come in response to the thirst for beauty and order. The language of Muse inspiration works with associations of moisture and creativity, of well springs, of flow, of flooding, of the ebb, with 'drying up'. Ancient Greek culture believed "...Muse inspired waters of creativity were as essential, as dangerous, as elemental, and as impossible to ignore as were the unpredictable waters of Mt. Helicon." [98] Perhaps this reverence for water and its qualities was amplified for the Greeks due to their literal dependence on water in the semi-arid geography of their own country. Such a landscape would give rise to water as metaphor, one that would also emphasize the soul's dependence on the "well springs" of Muse inspired arts.

Gaston Bachelard notes correspondences between water, the Muses, and spoken words. He suggests that the nature of language is aquatic; that liquidity is a primary principal of language since "...Human language has a liquid quality, a flow in its overall effect, water in its consonants. ... this liquidity causes a special psychic excitement that, in itself, evokes images of water." [99] For Bachelard water ways were sites for muse work, "...the stream will teach you to speak, in spite of pain and memories, it will teach you through euphoria and euphuism, energy through poems. Not a moment will pass without repeating some lovely, round words that rolls over stones." [100] To be "mused" is to look into a water mirror, to look "down and in," to court reverie, and to be amused.

Calliope "Hero stories, epic stories, poetic stories"

a) write about a time you met a hero, or were a hero to someone else

b) visit your personal history list; create an epic poem of that captures a portion of your life or an epic poem that honors your roots or heritage.

c) review your personal history list; write three poems;

☐ one to capture a precious past moment

☐ the second to capture the love of a friend

☐ the third to capture a powerful turning point in your life.

d) Play around with titles for each entry on your personal history list. Just brainstorm, don't censor your ideas. Don't be afraid to be silly. Try looking through a book of quotations or poetry for ideas. Create a list of chapter titles to guide you through and extended piece of writing.

e) Epics are driven by strong emotion; fear, love, hate. Every human being has experiences with these emotions.

Think about someone from your personal history list… (or if you are fearless, yourself)…what is this person afraid of? In love with? What does he/she loathe?

…Think back to a terrifying moment in your life—a car accident, a walk down an unlit street, a situation in which you were almost caught doing something wrong—describe the physical sensations you experienced. Write down the thoughts that went through your head at the time. Record any delayed reactions you had as well.

…Take a few minutes to think about something that terrified you when you were little. Write it from a child's point of view.

Polyhymnia

The muse Polyhymnia, "many hymns," is the sister whose realm of inspiration encompasses oral language, sacred hymns and poetry. She is often depicted as "pensive and veiled." [101] Her focus is on helping one find the sacred in the everyday, as well as on creating eloquent speech about those experiences. Through Polyhymnia, a memoirist finds moments of revelation and wonder, epiphanies of the mystery that lives us. Angeles Arrien describes this Muse as the one who "...is responsible for igniting all poets who touch the numinous, mystical, and inspirational realms." [102] Her influence is behind all forms of liturgical music, in all the ways human beings sing praise and express joy in the sacred mysteries. One can imagine Polyhymnia as a bridge between the sacred and the ordinary, as associated with a mode of communicating spiritual experiences.

One of the paradoxical qualities she evokes is silence; she helps us see how we can come to better understand the relationship between silence and expression. This Muse causes one to reflect quietly, to express without words what has been found in contemplation. The art of mime is an example of how such an expression of silence has been cultivated. Barbara Hort notes that Polyhymnia's particular gift in the process of re-membering a myth is the "capacity to stay silent–to hold ourselves still, contemplative, and receptive to the archaic Memory that seeks to be remembered."[103] In moments of silence one can listen most deeply for what has meaning for a person, as well as which sacred image wants now to be expressed in the world. Silence can also be a paradoxical byproduct of the urge to create; writer's block is a common response to the writer's agenda of completing a piece of writing. Polyhymnia can be imagined in these silences as well. She "challenges every artist to recognize that it is during silence of creative drought that the seeds of true art can gather strength–a strength sufficient to enable their fruit to triumph over the artist's overly earnest ego." [104]

Polyhymnia's form will present sacred epiphanies, simple language, and space on the page. The memoirist mused by her will understand the need for slowing the pace of the story, considering the reader's need to digest what has been set down. Polyhymnia reminds the writer of memoir about the importance of proceeding respectfully through a story and to give room for the reader to pause and consider the images recorded.

Writer, teacher, and Zen student Natalie Goldberg has long found relationship between the practice of Zen and writing. Her first book, *Writing Down the Bones,* was structured like a book of Zen teachings, *Zen Mind Beginner's Mind.* You can open the book at random and start with any section. It is an approach which honors silence and white spaces on a page. Goldberg's writing instruction has come to emphasize her teacher Katagiri Roshi's three main tenants: Continue under all circumstances, don't be tossed away, make positive effort for the good. Her approach has been compared to Julia Cameron's morning pages, which she describes in *The Artists' Way.* However, Goldberg's writing practice specifies timed writings; taking a topic and writing for ten minutes, twenty minutes, or an hour. In her memoir, *Long Quiet Highway,* Goldberg unfolds the story of her teacher Katagiri Roshi and her own study of Zen in Minnesota. She offers a metaphor for how one becomes a writer in her introduction;

There is an order of Buddhist monks in Japan whose practice is running. They are called the marathon monks of Mount Hiei. They begin running at one-thirty A.M. and run from eighteen to twenty-five miles per night, covering several of Mount Hiei's most treacherous slopes. Because of the high altitude, Mount Hiei has long cold winters, and part of the mountain is called the Slope of Instant Sobriety; because it is so cold, it penetrates any kind of illusion or intoxication. The monks run all year round. They do not adjust their running schedule to the snow, wind, or ice. They wear white robes when they run, rather than the traditional Buddhist black. White is the color of death: There is always the chance of dying on the way. In fact, when they run they carry with them a sheathed knife and a rope to remind them to take their life by disembowelment or hanging if they fail to complete their route. [105]

She goes on to say, "One becomes a writer by writing every day. Getting up in the middle of the night and running one's fingers over the keyboard for 25 miles. Writing as you cover the dangerous slopes of your inner being. Writing in the high elevations of your soul as the years pass by. Writing as the freezing winds, snow, and ice buffet you. Writing into sobriety as the cold loneliness of the keyboard penetrates your every illusion. Writing with the white robe of Death over your shoulders as He waits for you along the way." Metaphors are important to writers. She goes on to explain how writing practice can be a tool for slowing down and processing life experiences. "People would rather read about how to become a writer than read the actual products of writing: poems, novels, short stories. Americans see writing as a way to break through their own inertia and become awake, to connect with their deepest values. Yes, writing can do this for us, but becoming awake is not easy. One must be persistent under all circumstances and it is not always exciting. It is hard. It is a long quiet highway." She emphasizes the commitment we need to make our own way writing; "We, who are not marathon monks, wake up and have the toothbrush before us—brushing our teeth! The great ritual that gets us out of bed—and then we have the blank page in front of us, or the school bus, or the phone ringing. We all must go on down that highway. Our life is the path of learning, to wake up before we die."[106]

Goldberg has mastered what Polyhymnia offers: a form which contains sacred epiphanies, simple language, and space on the page. The memoirist mused by her will understand the need for slowing the pace of the story, considering the reader's need to digest what has been set down. Polyhymnia reminds the writer of memoir about the importance of proceeding respectfully through a story and to give room for the reader to pause and consider the images recorded

---

Polyhymnia Exercises:

a) **Describe an 'a-ha' moment of connection to something beyond yourself**

b) **Describe a place that sets you to reverie…**

c) **Write about an experience of solitude…**

d) **Write about the first time you ever saw a mime or pantomime performance**

e) **Work the experience of sounds into your writing. Revisit an episode from your personal history list. Take a minute to imagine what sounds might be going on in the background. Are there voices in the distance? Can you hear laughter? Crying? Whispering? Arguing? Are there any machines you can hear? A refrigerator humming? The bell of a cash register? The music or static coming from a radio or a particular T.V. program? Try to weave ore sounds into your work.**

f) **Create a Sacred Space for writing. Make your workspace into an altar, a sacred place where ideas and archetypes can act out their dramas. Put pictures of loved ones on your desk. Place a flower in a vase or an object of beauty in your sight line. … Your desk need not be neat—it need not be a desk at all—but make it a sacred spot that will entice your muse to visit.**

Melpomene

Texts shaped under the influence of Melpomene offer both recitations of tragedy and vehicles for processing grief. Her name harkens back to the Greek word *melpein,* meaning "to sing sacred songs of sorrow." Melpomene's area of inspiration is tragedy, a mode of story that portrays the deep conflicts of life experience.

The word tragedy comes from a melding of the Greek *tragos* and *aeiden*, translated as "goat-song." These associations go back to the first performance of tragedies in which, scholars believe, the chorus singers dressed in goat skins to honor Dionysus. The Greeks understood the importance of naming suffering and sorrow; for them the theater itself was a vehicle for community catharsis, for calling out the dark side of human nature and working through both catastrophic and daily events. Tragedy presents the reality of human suffering and allows the audience/reader to confront the incomprehensible questions of human existence within a cast of characters.

This mode of presentation evokes introspection: How am I like or unlike this person? How are the choices that were made like or unlike my own? What circumstances in my own life parallel this story? The point of such a mode of presentation is to use the power of grief and suffering to evoke healing within the community. Tragedy's medicine facilitates the recognition of flaws of character, mistakes in judgment, and failures in achievement. It calls the audience to assume personal responsibility for what one contributes to the suffering of the self and of the world.

Memoir shaped under Melpomene's influence will be writing informed by grief. Aurora Levins Morales underscores this point: "What does grief have to do with history? Everything." [107] She continues: "The only way to bear the overwhelming pain of oppression is by telling, in all its detail, in the presence of witness and in the context of resistance, how unbearable it is." [108] Melpomene's influence bears witness to suffering and grief. As a daughter of Mnemosyne, Melpomene remembers the grief of her own mother who witnessed the unbearable pain of her grandmother Gaia's repressed births. Carrin Dunne also notes the etymological connection of mourning and memory,

> Our English word "memory" can be traced to a single Proto-Indo-European root, *(S)mer,* to mourn. *(S)mer* can also mean "pith" or "marrow." ... As a verb it means to smear or apply salve. As pith or marrow, *(S)mer* suggests what we mourn for, what memory strives for, even if it can only be experienced as an absence, is indeed the center, the essence, the choicest

70

part. *(S)mer* as memory gives us the psychic (to mourn) and spiritual (to remember).[109]

Melpomene, a daughter of Goddess Memory, opens the way for mournful tellings, written out of tears and heartache, much like those found in the contemporary American music forms of Country Western honky-tonk, or the Blues. Her way of telling is through both the expression and evocation of grief.

Melpomene understands the power that a story be told is powerful precisely because it bears witness to suffering. She opens the way for mournful stories, written out of the wisdom of tears and heartache. Her way of shaping a story is through both the expression and evocation of grief. Writing memoir becomes one means of coping with such trauma. By describing the details of tragic event, a writer bears witness and causes the reader to consider his/her own relationships and experiences in light of this particular telling. The memoirist who chooses to re-tell traumatic experiences activates a process of cultural change, beginning with herself. It simultaneously creates both intimacy and distance with the story which presents itself.

If you are brave enough and ready, writing about a trauma can offer a particular window into the culture in which we live. Such narratives set in motion different questions. Writing about trauma in memoir form provides one way for a person to reconstruct her world view with the knowledge that evil can and does happen. It also creates opportunity for making peace with trauma by creating what Laura Brown describes as its "... painful knowledge into a new ethic of compassion, feeling with, struggling with the web of life in which they find themselves."[110] The memoirist who chooses to tell her traumas changes the culture from the inside out because she draws stories formerly from the margins into the center of discussion on human experiences.

Writer Louise DeSalvo affirms the connection between writing and the move toward restoring a sense of wholeness about the events of one's life. "Ultimately, then, writing about difficulties enables us to discover the wholeness of things, the connectedness of human experience. We understand that our greatest shocks do not separate us from human kind. Instead, through expressing ourselves, we establish our connection with others and with the world. " [111] Because Memory herself offers multiple ways of recalling an event, she introduces the quality of flexibility in dealing with traumatic events. It is this particular gift of flexibility which offers potential healing of a traumatic memory. "Memory is everything. Once flexibility is introduced, the traumatic memory starts losing its power over current experience. By imagining [these] alternative scenarios, many [writers] are able to soften the intrusive power of the original, unmitigated horror." [112] Flexibility allows one to shift perspectives, and as writer Mark Doty observes in his memoir *Heaven's Coast*, "What is healing but a shift in perspective?"

Writing personal narratives has helped many heal from the effects of loss, grief, personal tragedy by providing a vehicle which facilitates new ways of coping with life's challenges. Trauma carries its own kind of wisdom, and in its wake, new perspectives are born. DeSalvo asks writers to consider, "What if writing were a simple, significant, yet necessary way to achieve spiritual, emotional, and psychic wholeness? To synthesize thought and feeling, to understand how feeling relates to the events in our lives and vice versa?" [113] I wonder if writing hasn't been a way of healing since Hesiod first recorded the *Theogony*. I like to imagine Mnemosyne and her daughter Melpomene standing behind the impulse to write a particular life story, both helping to join the elements of thought, emotion, and body experience, elements broken apart by trauma.

Think about Mnemosyne's mythic associations and her relation-ship to the process of healing, of re-membering events into some-thing whole. She sets in motion several possibilities for healing; writing memoir as *imaginal healing* for both writer and reader; the possibility of *physiological healing*; and the expression of memoir as a *cultural healing* agent.

For many of us, September 11 2001 is a day that brought us abruptly into grief, causing a long period of mourning. The week after I wrote the following piece;

Even Terrorists Have Mothers
    No words. Horror. Images of destruction. Fireballs, explosions, huge buildings buckling and imploding. Death, so much death right before our eyes. I am numb from the staggering numbers. The stories

of last calls to family members pull in the pit of my stomach and my eyes well and spill over with each telling. Poignant photographs of smiling people who were here on last Tuesday morning and are now suddenly gone remind me of the Buddhist teaching of impermanence. How quickly, how unexpectedly life ends. Such a fragile enterprise this business of walking and breathing into each moment.

No longer a group of pseudo-innocents in the world community, America now joins the sorrowing ranks of those who know the pain of losing citizens to inexplicable acts of terror on her own soil. I can no longer pretend I live in a country which is invincible by virtue of technology and economic strength. It is now impossible to ignore the fact that as an American, there are those who would consider me an enemy. I have not chosen a vocation which requires intense global political savvy, yet I am now painfully aware that there are those who have played in this arena who embody greed and a thirst for superiority. The sobering light of a new day is here, a day which requires I explain hatred to my children. Hatred which led some other mother's sons to take vows of suicide in an attempt to draw attention to what our country has not wanted to see: people in the Middle East have been dying and displaced for the past twenty years and the U.S. has both fed the machines of war and offered humanitarian aid to the victims. The country in which we live is not easily explained to children. This recent act of terrorism isn't a simple black and white attack on freedom and democracy as the rhetoric makers have decried it; it is so much more complex. A web woven of promises and betrayals, a web America helped to weave. A web America now finds herself in the position of viewing through the aftermath's acrid and hazy air. What have we done? What will we do?

My daughter asks Why would anyone fly a plane full of ordinary people into a building in the middle of New York City? Why would anyone do such a thing on purpose? Why would anyone want to die like that? The questions keep coming. The answers are hard for me to grasp, let alone for my daughters and countless other children. In searching for answers, I try to explain how there are some people in the world who hate America, how America has hurt them. How when people let hate into their hearts it can take over and make them blind to the suffering of others. How by hating back only worsens the cycle by making hate stronger. Each human being has the ability to give into evil, and become overpowered by its force. We all do wrong, we all hurt others in our lives. The important thing is to recognize when I've hurt another, and then do what I can to heal the wrong. It is important to separate the people from the action. While I despise the acts of last week and all the suffering inflicted on thousands of innocent families, to hate those who committed these actions is to step into the abyss of hatred which had already swallowed them.

The actions of this past week have thrown me into a place of trying to explain good and evil to my nine-year-old, realizing it as a topic which has been grist for philosophers and theologians throughout human history. I am aware of the enormity of the questions and my own puniness. Martin Buber, a Jewish theologian, wrote an entire treatise on the topic, exploring the ideas of the innate human capacity for evil. He further explored an idea he called 'radical evil,' an overpowering persistence of evil, a state in which there is a refusal to see oneself as standing in any relation to any standard outside ourselves. It is a state of being likened to a vortex, a vortex which can swallow any human being who becomes overtaken by fears, resentments, and temptations. A vortex each of us is bound to come upon in our life, one which reminds us we have a choice of how to respond.

I struggle to see beyond the evil, to see the faces of the terrorists, to remember even they had mothers and families who must also be struggling to make sense of their own grief and rage. I want my children to understand revenge is not healthy. I want them to be strong enough not to hate back, yet clear-eyed enough to know when to step away from danger. I pray for peace, like so many others in the world, knowing life has always been fragile enterprise.

Reverie Reverence Revelation

It has been six weeks since the terrorist attacks. Each new Tuesday morning has settled into a Tuesday mourning. I light a single candle on my kitchen counter and stand at the abyss of grief that cracked open that day in lower Manhattan. The names of those who have died and those who have survived continue to appear before us in print, photographs, video. The ache of loss is in my bones. I have learned to turn off the news in the morning. Our country's response to Afghanistan both sickens and disheartens me. So much violence. So many children without parents, so many orphans already.

In trying to make sense of the chaos of recent events I have found myself reflecting on the inter-relatedness of the one and the many. I have glimpsed the pattern of the collective culture in the singleness of my own life. In a fractal way, September had already been a month of losses, a month marking anniversaries of sorrow. It is the month in which my father was born in the 1930s to my then eighteen-year-old grandmother. He was the first child born to my grandparents, the result of youthful impatience and the Lutheran imperative to 'do the right thing,' born just nine month shy of their December engagement. They were not prepared to be parents, but who ever is? When he was just a week old, he caught a cold which quickly turned to a croup. Steam tenting was recommended, a much more primitive affair than what we have now a days. There was an accident. His legs were burned so badly that he had to spend the next six months in the children's ward at the hospital in St. Paul. Eventually infection set in and both of his legs had to be amputated just below the knee. Grief and guilt loomed large. I wish I could say things got better for my father, that he had a family who closed ranks and resolved to help him make his life the best it could be, but they didn't. My grandfather was terribly ashamed. He could hardly tolerate the sight of his oldest son and his two wooden legs. Such grief. My father died when he was forty-four, the age I will be in the coming year. He never visited New York; I think the farthest he ever traveled was to Minnesota, the year he went to live with relatives because of the animosity at home. He loved cars and eventually became a mechanic, making a life out of repairing engines and pounding out dented fenders. He lived life on his own terms and died from lung cancer, a casualty of a two-pack-a-day addiction. His legacy to me has been the kind of gold grief yields: a familiarity with loss, regret, and Milton's "sense of tears in mortal things."

Why does this come to me now as I try to cope with the senseless violence of the world around me? I suppose because I have lived with the reverberations of violence in my own family, the place a person expects to be the most secure. September is a month which holds the soil of well tilled personal sorrows, and I have found room here for the events of September 11th. In trying to cope with the enormity of loss inflicted on so many unsuspecting people in the midst of their most ordinary work days, I have found it helpful to let the candle's flame guide my reveries on grief. In these moments, I wander to the places of old wounds and find to my relief, it is familiar territory with a path of well worn stones. The recent terrorist attacks have given each of us the opportunity to stop and reflect on the gifts of grief and cultivating a more compassionate heart. There is a place in my chest that has held great grief, and while life has continued to flow around and through me, this place in my chest was hollowed out at an early age. The recent tragedies of our world find a place to settle here. In an odd way, the wounds of my father have become a source of strength. The scarred place in my soul has become a place for tending grief, knowing evil has come and will come again. I have lived to witness its presence and to add my voice to the chorus of survivors. Life is precious, each moment. As I light my candle each quiet Tuesday morning, I recall the gifts of grief and the poignancy of each life, woven with its unique thread into the tapestry of the human community.

And a year later, this:

Can it be a whole year has passed since the horror of the events which unfolded from 9/11? The images from that day live just behind my eyelids and in the pit of my stomach, all too easily activated whenever travel plans are part of daily life. The face of Osama bin Laden is known by even the youngest children in our community, thanks to the media blitz of fault-finding and finger-pointing which has ensued. The United States had the opportunity to demonstrate alternative behavior, not to jump immediately to force, but old ways of thinking, like old habits, die hard in this country, it seems. I had hoped we had learned something from our last "wars." It is apparent we have not. Once the force of the war machine is unleashed, we seem to be hard pressed to stop its blind fury. We are like the Cyclops who has had its only eye put out. Afghanistan, a country of little means and little defense was attacked with the full force of the U.S. military. An Israeli-American friend of mine described our actions as "squadron bombing a peanut butter sandwich in the desert."

How have such actions profited us or the world? Our government seeks to assure us that without these extended military actions the Taliban would still be in control, its women and children still being treated as chattel, abused and deprived of the most basic of human decencies. None of us wants to be contributing to the suffering of women and children, but how many more have we caused to suffer by killing their fathers, brothers, uncles, cousins? Who will be left to care for those on whose behalf we claim to make war?

Meanwhile, back here in the States, most of us have gotten on with our lives. Our children went back to school, we went back to work, celebrated our holidays, took our vacations. Some of us had family members who were called to active duty with reserve forces like the National Guard, some of us had family members who were actually called away for tours of duty. But most of our soldiers have come home safely, replaced by those who have been assigned the next rotation of a 'button pushing' war. Our forces are so over-prepared relative to their Afghani targets that casualties for us become unexpected. It seems we have forgotten that in wars people die on both sides.

I have conflicting emotions these days at the sight of so much red white and blue. Our family celebrated the 4th of July in an All American venue; we went to a baseball game in our community's newly built baseball stadium. The flags were everywhere, the Star Spangled Banner was sung by a teacher from the community, children from various service organizations led the flag salute from home plate. The moment that will not leave me was this: as the teacher came to the last few bars of the national anthem, two fighter jets swooped low from the sky, streaking a neat diagonal over the field. The crowd went wild. The sound of cheering, whistles, clapping reverberated off the walls for a good five minutes. Tears streamed down my face. I could not help but think of the irony of the spectacle. We could cheer at the sight of F-16's, at the deafening roar they trailed, but what about the people half a world away in Afghanistan? Such sights surely invoke sheer terror and chaos, portents of greater destruction. What are we teaching our children when we celebrate instruments of war with such joy?

How has my life changed since the events of September 11? I have come to news reports with a more jaded eye, suspecting that our current administration lacks both the intelligence and the ethics to implement the difficult and complex path required of peace makers. I hesitate to travel, not because I fear for my safety more than previously, but because I have been reminded of life's fragile and transient nature. I am more conscious of teaching tolerance. I am more aware than ever that in order to create a tolerant culture, adults—who have the *capacity to recognize and respect the beliefs and practices of others—must raise up children who value tolerance. And, I grieve. While I know the value of grief, that over time it becomes the gold, the thing of most value with the passage of time, I struggle with the enormity of it all. I am comforted by the words of Eli Wiesel:*

> *"To forget nothing, to efface nothing: that is the obsession of survivors; to plead for the dead, to defend their memory and honor......So some of us weave these words into tales, stories, and pleas for memory and decency. It is all we can do for the living, and for the dead."*

Waking each day and walking through it require us to find our courage and what it is that sources our hopes. For myself, I look in the eyes of my children.

Melpomene Exercises:

a) Write about a loss...first awareness of mortality... disappointment with an important person...a deep personal hurt...

b) Write about your sources of comfort/inspiration during difficult times

c) ...a story of forgiveness...

d) ...a story of compassion in response to tragedy...

e) ...read the obituaries, find a story, write a eulogy for a real or fictional character

f) Think about particular rituals you have experienced. Rituals help create boundaries of time and place and help us fully engage our emotions. They help us shift gears, make transitions, and help adjust our mental states to big changes. We engage in small rituals everyday; those daily rituals that help us wake up, as well as those that help us go to sleep. Are there any rituals from your personal history list that stand out? Birth stories? Religious rituals? Funerals/Memorials?

Terpsichore

Terpsichore's name is translated as "whirler" and she is described as "she who loves to dance." Texts shaped under her influence come out of the body, emphasizing kinesthetic memory and sensibility as the very foundation of story. This muse encourages the use of the body as authentic vehicle for expressing internal and external experiences. Much of the work done by Jungian analyst Marian Woodman draws from the idea of the body's inherent intelligence and creativity. She has spent years developing workshops designed to aid participants in recognizing the connections between psyche and body. Her focus has been one to call women to recognize the strong emotions that are embedded in the very musculature of the body. Using dream images, Woodman encourages women to associate these images to particular parts of the body and watch for changes both in the image and in the body. [114] Another key component of Woodman's style of "body work" involves the recovery of voice, both metaphorically and literally. She encourages women to release the muscles in the torso, throat and hips in order to feel their voice emerging at its most natural register. Her work recognizes how the human body is imprinted by memories of a life, by both pleasurable and painful events. The body itself holds the stories of a life. For a memoirist, the body becomes a tactile/sensory encyclopedia, a repository of experiences which serve as the foundation of her stories.

The association of women writers and the body has been explored by a variety of feminist writers, including Adrienne Rich, who describes the relationship this way:

> When I write "the body," I see nothing in particular. To write "my body" plunges me into lived experience, particularity: I see scars, disfigurements, discolorations, damages, losses, as well as what pleases me. ...To say "the body" lifts me away from what has given me a primary perspective. To say "my body" reduces the temptation to grandiose assertions. [115]

Another aspect of Terpsichore's musing is that of dance, a creative joining of body and rhythm. Joan Stroud describes dance as "... the liminal space—the punctuation between stillness and activity, between gravity and freedom, between transience and permanence. To dance is to define the center...the dancer dances formlessness into form"[117] ; each gesture conveys an emotion that is part of a larger story. For the memoirist, this muse inspires one to consider both choreography and movement. She inspires the collection of sensory memory fragments and dancing them into the form of a story. How does a text dance? What are the rhythms of the story, where in the body does this story live? Terpsichore asks the memoirist to consider her body, to allow it to bring forward the images and sequences of movement which have long been silent.

Marion Woodman writes powerfully in journal form of her confrontation with uterine cancer in her memoir titled *Bone: Dying Into Life.* She details the factors she feels played a role in her illness, and how she comes to treat and tend her body. Using dreams and imagery, self-reflection and body work, both traditional and alternative medicines are incorporated into her treatment regime. She engages in intense self-questioning, "What does it mean to be an elder in this culture? What has to be let go of? Do I have the courage to live?" Her journey not only culminates in a return to well being, but also in an acceptance of both life and death, a lesson central to any healing process.

As a dancer and teacher who has worked her whole life to demonstrate how the psyche and body are related, she receives an affirmation of health in the form of a dance. The following excerpt is the final entry in *Bone*, a fitting conclusion to this poignant journey:

April 1, 1995

"Let's dance."

"Oh, Marion," he says, "you know you can't dance. You could break your back."

I sit out the polka, can't keep my feet still. They remember— oh how they remember tapping it out in South Porcupine, Timmins, Schumacher, Heidelberg, Rüdesheim, Grinzing, yes, even Old London. I feel like Death sitting there with all my life past. Then my hands are clapping like a child's. The energy builds, becomes so fierce I feel like a puppet with hands and feet tapping syncopated rhythms, feet doubling in toe and heel. Puppet becomes young woman, vibrant with animal energy. A voice comes up from my perineum, "Marion, you can sit on this couch until you rot, but I am going to dance. I don't care what Ross thinks. I don't care what these Dutch-Canadians think. I don't care what anybody thinks. I don't care if you break your back. I don't care if you drop down dead. I am going to dance! I am going to live!" I feel the archetypal energy lifting me off the couch, propelling me across the room—I feel it pushing through my benumbed feet, legs, thighs, torso, arms, hands, through every cell into my head. It is TOTAL. I feel myself Gypsy—a twenty-four-year-old glowing woman. I am being danced. People are gazing at me aghast, probably thinking, "This old lady sat on the couch all evening; suddenly she's transformed into a hands-in-the-air gypsy. What's she up to?" Do I care?

I become concentration. Then a stranger—a Dutchman who has just arrived—catches my vision, jumps into my circle, and we dance a dance as fierce as I have never danced before. If my back breaks, if I drop dead, it doesn't matter. I am twenty-four. I am healthy. I am whole. [118]

Terpsichore Exercises:

a) Write about the first time you remember dancing...

b) Write about a time you saw your parents dance...

c) Describe your relationship to movement...have you ever had dance lessons?

d) The first time you saw a dance performance...ballet... modern...ethnic...

e) Your awareness of the variety of rhythms and what each calls out of your body...

f) Your experience with sports...exercise...gym class... yoga...

g) A quote from the movie, Chariots of Fire, " ...when I run, I feel His pleasure."

Describe a moment when participating in movement of you body connected you to something larger than yourself.

Thalia

Thalia is the muse who inspires comedy; whose presence inspires the resolution of opposites in the juxtaposition of discord with dialogue. She is the muse who prods consideration of alternatives when confronted with polarities and paradoxes. Her name is derived from the Greek *thallen,* meaning "flourishing," etymologically drawing associations of robust health and prosperity with humor. Comedy reminds us about community and living in harmony with others, especially with those whom we deem different from ourselves. Mary Lou Hoyle affirms that "Comedy teaches us how to live... lends itself to celebrations of inclusion and completion; comedy celebrates at the appropriate time, when the furious activity of living reaches a concluding moment, and these songs include the whole community." [119] The comic is aimed at reconciliation, at bringing together otherwise disparate entities. Comedy encourages the ability to laugh at one's self, to allow for role reversals, and to invite participation. "Comedy includes its audience as part of its action. It is the true expression of democracy, of and by the people. Comedy is spontaneous and can... erupt when it is unintended. ...Thalia appears when a people, as a people, need release from the bondage of law, the rigidity of custom, or from simple self-importance." [120] There are times in all life stories when the weight of experience can threaten to extinguish the desire to continue the journey. The Muse of comedy knows when it is the right time to loosen our grip and lighten our load by laughing out loud.

Author Tristine Rainer understands the necessity of humor in writing memoir: "It's an antidote to bragging, a light that illuminates the ugly and subhuman, a salve for corrosive anger, a remedy for the lasting pain of embarrassment." [121] Telling a story with humor helps us shift to a new perspective, encourages playfulness in the face of heavy circumstances. Thalia is the muse who celebrates breaking form; the poignancy of a coming of age story or a story of a first love is touched by her when the writer remembers moments in the episode which caused great embarrassment or didn't go the way they were expected. She encourages the memoirist to laugh at herself, to make fun of her own foibles, and by so doing extend the opportunity to the reader as well. A comic view of life is important because comedy offers its own form of wisdom, valuable for its honesty and lack of pretentiousness. Comedy makes room for questions, for spontaneity, and for play. Comedy asks the question, "What if?" and doesn't flinch from showing us ourselves in moments when we were less than perfect.

In a recent *New Yorker* piece, "Tales from a Chelsea Soup Kitchen," humorist Ian Frasier, describes how he started a writing workshop that operates in tandem with a NYC church-based soup kitchen. In a later interview he describes his thoughts on writing humor:

Sometimes people write funny things and I say, you know if you just made it a little longer and added a little plot, you'd have a humor piece here. It isn't just people in this workshop. It's people in general. They'll get something funny, but it'll just be a line or two lines. Even now I think because of TV I think that's become a problem—that people write really,

really short. So all of the suggestions of where this could go, you know there's all this potential here.

[Humor] is something that you really can't hit by aiming at it. It's not like you can go out and get the facts and report them and now here's a humor piece with the facts. With reporting, if you work hard you can usually pull something out. But writing humor doesn't respond to working hard, necessarily. I mean, you could just sit there and look at the page all day and maybe something will come. But writing humor for me is more like a watchful-ness. You have to watch. When you say something funny, or someone else does, it's more like you wait for the piece. I think maybe it's more like writing a poem. I've never really been into that at all, but I assume a poet would get to a certain point and say, gee, I know I need a fifth stanza here, but I don't know what it should be. And then maybe the poet doesn't think of anything for five years. I don't know I can imagine that; I've had it happen with humor pieces. I'll get to a certain point and say, you know, up to here it works but I don't know what to do next. It's a sense—you have a sense of humor. [122]

Should you decide to court the Muse of Humor, here are "The Three Things That Make You Funnier (and Better) Than Regular People Who Aren't As Funny As You," according to columnist Howard Leff:

1. Voice

2. Attitude

3. Tone

OK, four.
4. Originality.

He says, "Successful humor writers, like all comic writer/performers, possess these qualities and know how to use them. This doesn't always 'just happen' organically." Even Erma Bombeck one of the most famous American Humorists in recent history said humor writing is just like all writing; you have to sit down and put pen to paper or finger to keyboard. Everyday. It takes discipline.

It also takes courting Thalia; find out what she likes and put it on your desk or writing nook. Find something whimsical that makes you smile. I have a collection of plastic wind up toys in my desk drawer. My favorite is a red mouse with a piece of plastic cheese that does bunny hops. He makes me laugh even though his hops are getting slower than when I first found him.

One of my current favorite humorists is Nora Ephron. She has written literate and funny screenplays for "When Harry Met Sally" and "Heartburn." Her understated wit has punctured many a bubble of conformity and made audiences laugh in recognition. When her latest book arrived, the title made me smile with a bit of recognition: *I Feel Bad About My Neck.* She called our attention to a new body part to agonize over, one the beauty magazines haven't caught up with (yet!). Below is a column I wrote for our local paper last year on the occasion of a birthday I wasn't quite really for, but humor helped!

Time Marches and Gravity Happens

Ta-da! Thanks to another year without any major accidents or illnesses, my body has managed to get me through to my next birthday.

This year is the year I have turned fifty years old.

I have been looking in the mirror a lot these past few months. While I have much for which to be grateful, I do have a few protests:

- *My hair is receding at the temples just like my father's did. I feel like I just have to say, Wait a minute, I am a woman and this is just not what I was prepared for. I mean, a little gray hair, a little salt and pepper I can deal with, but hair loss? Come on!*
- *O.K., it's not just the hair thing ...my cheeks are falling. Yes, it's true, my cheeks are falling. What used to be round and wholesome is drooping in more places that it's polite to mention in mixed company. I used to think plastic surgery was a ridiculous self indulgence. On my last visit to the dermatologist, she gently broached the subjects of Botox, Juvederm and Restilin. She used words like 'lift', 'freshen' and 'soften.' Like I am a pillow*

> *that needs a good fluffing. And that was just my face. These days I am less judgmental of Joan Rivers and friends.*

* *Then there was the whole move from the previously helpful under-wire bra to POWER SHAPERS. I get it now, who REALLY wants to see which upper body part reaches our navel first?*

* *I have become a Spanx convert. (Gentlemen, if you don't know what these are, go ahead and let your mind wander. I'm sure it will be more entertaining than the reality of reduced circulation and another condition we ladies call 'muffin-top.') The idea is to 'lift' and 'firm' one's hips, thighs, and torso. They don't tell you what gets firmed one place is just displaced higher up where spandex ends and skin begins. Oh for a pair of jeans and the Way I Was. I haven't just suffered through 'muffin top,' I have endured multiple push-up 'popovers' too. While all this has given me new sympathies for the Pillsbury dough boy, at least he can still laugh when someone pokes him in his fluffy middle. Come to think of it, you never see him trying to stuff himself in a new pair of Levi's do you?*

* *My smile is definitely showing my caffeine intake more than it used too. It now takes three cups to wake up in the morning when it was only one or two a few years back. I have tried those whitening strips, but they make my teeth hurt. My dentist says tooth sensitivity increases with age. Thanks. I guess I should just be thankful I have teeth?!*

* *When I look in the mirror I see my father's face in female form...Now I am musing the merits of Pantene ProV versus Paul Mitchell... a total color job or whether or not a simple hair weave would be a good idea... (and I wonder, do real women use Rogaine?)*

Thalia Exercises:

a) a funny story from your childhood...

b) a family incident that is retold over and over because it makes people laugh

c) a favorite comedian...

d) a favorite comic strip...

e) a favorite play/movie ...are there particular scenes that make you laugh each time you see them?

f) A time when laughter shifted a tension...

g) A time when laughter wasn't expected, but helped weave a sense of community in the moment...

h) Family jokes...knock-knock jokes...why did the x cross the street jokes...

i) Take a look at your bookshelves and find another reference book to use for inspiration. Pick a page at random from an atlas and write a poem about that place. Open an encyclopedia and write a love song mentioning the first topic on the left-hand page. Pull a name from the phone hook and write a description of that person's living room. None of this has to be for publication, it is simply a way to get loosened up and have a little fun.

Euterpe

The muse Euterpe has long been associated with the flute, presiding over festivals and entertainments with such instruments as the panpipe or syrinx. She was often associated with shepherds, rustics, and common folk. Her name means "giver-of-pleasure," which was explained in Diodorus Siculus 4.7.1 thus: "...because she gives those who hear her sing delight (*terpein*) in the blessings which education bestows."[123] Euterpe was associated with the musical instrument that the Greeks called *aulos,* meaning "of the body's breath." Robert Dupree points out that the association to the flute was incorrect, that the *aulos* was actually a form of double reed instrument, much like the oboe.[124] Because of its relation to the body, *aulos* became associated with ecstasy, unreason, simultaneously divine and ordinary. The *aulos* also conjured sexuality because of its "...dramatic, emotional; versatile in mood and effect, capable of blaring vigor, plangent lamentation or sensual suggestiveness, [it] was used to create vivid and diverse forms of 'representation'." [125] The relationship of *aulos* to breath works as a kind of sound image of the human body, evoking vitality and movement. Euterpe will cause a text to evoke breath: catching one's breath, taking breath away, holding breath, letting breath go, sighing.

A memoir mused by Euterpe will display warmth, earthiness, sensuality, and like those mused by Terpsichore, a sense of the body. This muse asks the memoirist to consider both breath and tone. A memoir which considers the influence of tone will convey a sense of aliveness, passion, and immediacy. It will resonate with the reader, taking tones that reverberate. Zuckerkandl observes that tones unite, and that "...what tone expresses is not the subject but the interpenetration of a subject and an object." [126] The tone of the memoir is the means by which the reader finds herself affected, drawn in, and somehow, opened up. Euterpe encourages the art of listening; listening to the rhythm of the words, phrases, sentences, the overtones and undertones of the story itself. Her gift is in crafting a text with the capacity for resonance. The interpenetration is accomplished in relationship of the writer and reader. The memoirist finds her voice, tells her unique story and bears witness to the meaning one makes of a life. The listener/reader takes in the stories, recognizes glimmers of similar moments, and finds a moment of companionship.

When you consider the influence of tone, your story will provide a sense of aliveness, passion, and immediacy. It will resonate with the reader, taking tones which reverberate. Euterpe is the muse who encourages careful listening, for turning inward, and tracing evocative reverberations to the place of their beginnings. Below is a piece of my own memoir which I imagine Euterpe standing over my shoulder. It recounts a time when I lived outside Copenhagen as a high school exchange student.

Finnedalsvej, 1975

It was mid November. The days were gray and the winter rains had set in. This next family, the Norregaards, lived in a quiet suburb of Copenhagen. Here the houses were set back off the streets and away from heavy traffic. The street was called Finnedalsvej, and the house was a spacious single-story situated on a rectangular lot. The front was lined by a narrow drive way, with a prim green hedge outlining the house. It felt as new and modern as the home on Amager Landevej had been family-worn and traditional. Arnold was an advertising executive for a large firm in Copenhagen and recently active in the Rotary Club's International Exchange program. He was a small, trim man who was always impeccably dressed in gray flannel trousers. Ingrid, his wife, was a middle school teacher, and spoke beautiful British English. She was tall and thin, with wide eyes, and prominent teeth. They had two children, Nils, who was three years older than me, and Susanne, who was two years younger.

Ingrid was the most striking women I had ever met. She was fond of cognac and cigars. I had never seen a woman smoke cigars before, and I tried not to stare. My mother's father had smoked them when I was small, and the odor conjured memories of him meeting us at the train station. The smoke clung to his hat and his sweater. One of my earliest recollections of how a man smelled. Not a woman. Ingrid smoked when she relaxed alone at the table, staring out the window. Held gently between her thumb and forefinger, somehow she transformed the stubby brown roll into the essence of sophistication.

The first time I saw her, she caught me out of the corner of her eye, trying not to notice the thick stump between her fingers. She broke into a smile.

"Not used to seeing a lady smoke?" She laughed with her head back, enjoying my shock and discomfiture.

"Not to worry, we Danish women, we are real ladies, and we aren't concerned about what others think. Only with finding the pleasure of the moment. And this cigar," she waved her hand in conversation, "this cigar is a fine moment." The smoke wafted through the room and curled into my nose and mouth. Tickling, tempting me to believe in its powers of sensory expansion. But the smoke was too thick, too pungent, too insistent. I laughed back.

"No one back home will ever believe me anyway!"

When she was finished, she carefully stubbed out the remains in a tiny brass saucer. She carried it to the kitchen and immediately put it out with the trash.

"Nothing worse than the smell of a good moment that has passed," she joked, but she was fastidious about neatness in her home. There was no clutter, the edges of the furniture were bold and spare, light streamed through undraped windows during the day. The table in the dining room was a bare rectangle of oiled birch, and was framed by a view of the front entry, its low green hedge, and the street beyond. I had never experienced such clean lines. Light and shadow danced in long, lean patterns on the living room floor. Even the carpet was sheared with elegant low pile. It was quiet. I was still not used to the quiet. When I shut my eyes and thought about my brothers and sisters back home, the constant chatter and bickering of their voices was always present. The stark lines made me more aware of the sharp edges of my heart, the empty places, my loneliness.

Music was a keen interest in this family. Arnold loved classical concertos, Ingrid preferred operas, Nils lived for jazz and contemporary pop music. When Arnold realized I knew very little of the language of melody, he told me about the local music library and encouraged me to get a loaner card. A short bike ride from the house, at Tarnby Torv, it was a two story building made of cement and glass. Bleak on the outside, the same architectural style as the gymnasium. But inside, the walls were covered with posters of albums, artists, concerts. Chaotic color and disarray. Music leaked out the edges of doors where people could listen to albums before they checked them out. It spilled out over the sound system, quiet one moment, loud the next. The woman at the front desk was pleased to help me get my card, happy to meet an American. She asked where I was from and what brought me here, smiling with kind curiosity. Most of the kids in my class thought it was just plain odd that someone their age would choose to live so far away from home for a whole year. How could I leave my family, my friends, my life like that? I had gotten pretty good at answering those kind of questions. To see the world, to speak another language, to find the common denominators in our cultures. Aware of what I could never really say. To escape. Our conversation was much the same. She was older than me, in her twenties, and dressed in loose layers of worn cotton sweaters. Her skin glowed, her hair was wiry and curled out from the edges of the kerchief she knotted like a cap. I found myself staring at her every time I dropped by. An odd attraction I had never felt before. Butterflies. My mouth was dry when I spoke to her. I wondered if she noticed my eyes on her sweater, her soft round breasts, the curve of her cheek. Her smile and wave in my direction left me warm in places I tried not to think about.

I checked out record albums, week after week, indulging myself in stacks of popular music. John Croce, Gordon Lightfoot, David Gates, Bread, The Eagles, Cat Stevens, Three Dog Night, John Denver. I learned the names of songs, of albums, of record labels. Luxury. Record albums had not ever been something I could afford to buy, the money I earned had always gone for clothes and practical things. Now was my chance to play catch up. I went after school every Friday to choose new albums to borrow for the following week. Arnold showed me how to use his stereo equipment. There were head phones so I could plug in and listen in the den, I could close my eyes and be swept up in the golden guitar chords and story songs. The music gave me something else to talk about with Nils. He loved his records, and knew all the songs on both sides of every album he owned. When he recognized the Music Library bags appearing in the den, he began to invite me down to his room in the cellar of the house to listen to music with his friends on Friday nights. He poured wine in juice glasses and we sat on the floor, propped up with pillows, taking turns listening to each other's favorite songs and favorite albums. It was cozy in the candlelight, the conversation earnest and full of youthful assertions and enthusiasms.

"This is a fine song. The rhythm is the best. Listen."

Nils would put the record on his stereo, and place the needle down on a spot midway through the record. As if he knew every single audio line on the album, which one would begin the song he wanted us to hear. His accuracy was amazing, especially after so many glasses of wine. I would listen, sip, listen, sip, speak if spoken to, but listen mostly. My lips would tingle from the alcohol, and it became easier for me to smile. I liked his friends. They went out of their way to ask my opinions about music and how I was finding my stay in Denmark. Pia was a girl from across the street and was 2 years ahead of me at Tarnby Gym, Jens an old classmate of Nils from Reale Skole, and Jorgen, was another friend who had just come back from Holland after working as a watchmaker's apprentice. If I mispronounced a word, they just asked me to repeat myself. I grew comfortable in my corner and looked forward to seeing them all week by week. Their smiles were easy and comfortable, the kind that left me feeling warm inside.

Euterpe Exercises:

a) Listen to your favorite music…what images emerge?

b) Do you remember a piece of music from your childhood? Was it a lullaby? A song? Instrumental? Can you close you eyes and hear it now? What feelings does it evoke?

c) Write a story of a time a piece of music touched you deeply

d) Write a story of the role of music in your family of origin…

e) If you play/ed a musical instrument/sing; write about the process of learning;

Who was your teacher? When did you perform? What kept you going? Is there a particular performance that stands out in your memory?

Urania

Urania is the muse whose realm was designated as the study of the stars and astronomical writings. Her name comes from the Greek, *Ouranos* meaning heavenly, evoking her lineage to her maternal grandfather. By the time of Plato she was more specifically associated with the areas of astrology and astronomy, and by the era of Scientific Enlightenment she became a figure who symbolized rational intelligence.[127] Urania is the muse who inspires new discoveries, insights, inventions, and "aha" moments. She is responsible for evoking both curiosity and wonder, for provoking imaginal possibilities, and for motivating action to pursue what calls us. Robert Sardello points out that Urania is concerned with cosmological imagination, her unique musing frees the human mind from literal understandings of the sun, moon, and stars.[128]

Under her influence, cosmology becomes more than mere history; it becomes a metaphor for human life. Her way of musing encourages "soft eyes" in imagining the cosmos, that which is above and beyond us. The stories of the stars then allow us to imagine ourselves, all that lies within us. She corresponds to the concave mirror, the surface that draws us in to relationship with the transcendent. She motivates our pursuit of questions that will take us beyond what we already know, who ignites our desire to seek answers to ancient questions of humanity: Are we alone? Why do we suffer? Is there a God? Why do we dream? What is love, evil, death, hope? How should we live? Urania' helps us make the correspondences between inner and outer; to take in the patterns of the heavens, and to contemplate the possibility of a numinous order of things, not just out in the vast expanse of the cosmos, but within our own psyche as well.

Robert Sardello imagines her kind of musing as exemplified by the music of praise. He observes that musicians and astrologers of the Renaissance related the Muses to the nine choirs of angels, notes of the musical scales, mode of song, and levels of inspiration including body, soul, and spirit. Sardello maintains a Uranian imagination is one that "...can be seen as oriented toward or coming from praise." [129] He continues describing the relationship of the sound of praise to silence:

> The earthly world is the exact mirror image of the heavenly world. In the heavens, sound is outside silence. In the earthly world, sound is inside the silence of things. In the song of praise the silence of the world is taken to its homeland—all that is inside is transformed into outside. And that I think is the essence of praise. Nothing is held back, held in, kept quiet. In the song of praise the secret is let out, and the secret is that the earth is a spiritual world, but that secret can be revealed only in letting it out in praise. [130]

Urania grants the ability to see deeply without and within. The effect of such a gift is the perception of grace, which in turn evokes gratitude, and such gratitude draws forth praise. This Muse reminds us of both joy and humility.

A memoir shaped by Urania attempts to express the big questions as well as moments of personal clarity. It expresses the double-lensing quality of both macro and micro scopes, working the relationships between the inner and outer worlds metaphorically. The memoirist attempts to set down the correspondences between her daily experiences and the patterns she observes in the natural world, much like a naturalist. The naturalist's job is to observe and record phenomena and from there to make inference and interpretation. The memoirist working under Urania's influence will not be content with Clio's desire to record the facts; instead she will strive to look for the metaphor that lies below the experience. Once the metaphor has been constructed, she will continue the reverie for a glimpse of the presence of the Sacred and include this in her text. As Robert Sardello notes, Urania will inspire a text that will sing the praises of life and Dylan Thomas' "the force that through the green fuse drives the flower." Such writings will express both humility and awe in face of the ordinary and extraordinary moments of a life.

Spring Portents

The weather where I live belies the tension in the world as our government is still waging war in two countries. Casualty reports are no longer front page news, but young soldiers are still coming home to be buried. The rains have come, not as plentiful as we had hoped for, but there is snow in the mountains and the promise of at least one more good storm before the Ides of March. Daffodils are up in the front flower bed, their bright yellow faces the first signs of spring, as the neighborhood trees begin to bud and leaf out. The hummingbirds are still here, but they won't be for long. Every year at this time, just after we have passed the coldest of our weather, they take off for warmer parts and don't return until June around the Summer equinox. Their behavior puzzles me, and after living here these eleven years, I continue to wonder why they wait until after the freezing cold to leave. This is the best time of year here in the valley: the days are gentle and sunny, the flowers at their first-of-season best scent and color. There must be deeper song lines in their blood, ones my ears can't hear, that call them elsewhere. Hummingbirds remind me there will always be things I don't know, things I'll never understand. That being able to say "I don't know" isn't a failure, but an honest acknowledgment that comes with being human.

I don't know why my mother-in-law, the youngest of her family, developed Alzheimer's. I don't know why my father, the eldest in his family, had to die at the age of forty-four from lung cancer. I don't know what happens to the soul after the body dies, though I would like to believe it is present somewhere. I don't know why human kind is so easily led into the rhetoric and practice of war, despite our awareness of the horrors, of the grisly and senseless loss of life it brings. I don't know when or if we will ever learn peace as a species, though I know in my bones that we can't give up the vision. I don't know why I get to wake up in sunshine with food to eat in my cupboards while half way around the world, my women kin in Afghanistan must devote their every energy to making shelter and finding whatever they can to keep hunger at bay. I don't know.

What I know for sure at this point in my life is that there are no simple answers. We live in a complex set of relationships within our communities, our countries, and with the earth herself. Every action takes place within the web of global relationships; we can no longer afford the luxury of the illusion of independent decisions. The food I buy and the kind of vehicle I drive impacts my culture and my world from the inside out. Change begins with one small decision at a time.

What am I hoping to teach my daughters? That life is precious. And so is clean air and water. That the pursuit of things cannot bring happiness. That consciousness is a life-long endeavor, and that when we know better our charge is to do better. That being a peacemaker begins within oneself, one's family, one's community. That good, the evidence of love in the world, is stronger than evil. That the stories we tell both mirror and guide us. That living with paradox is part of life.

I made fresh nectar for the hummingbirds this morning. It is a ritual of nurture I enjoy, boiling water, stirring in the granulated sugar until it changes from milky white to crystal liquid. I stopped adding red food coloring several years ago when I learned it could weaken their eggshells. The loss of color in their food didn't phase them; they still come to the feeder, attracted by the red circular perches, and out of habit, I suppose. I am grateful for their company. When they light at the feeder just outside our dining room window, I am reminded that even hummingbirds with their soft blur of wings, stop and rest. I am also reminded how the smallest among us can teach us what it means to be fully present. I may not know where our hummingbirds go, but I have faith in their wise song lines. They will be back with more lessons, more reverie for me in the year ahead. In the meantime, I pray for Peace among all people. I pray for consciousness for those who would lead us down the OtherPath.

Urania Exercises:

a) 'what lies above and beyond also lies within'...
   Write a description of a place in nature and
   reflect how it speaks to you...

b) Write a story of star gazing...first time you
   recognized a constellation...

c) Write a story of wonder in the face of a natural
   phenomenon...

d) Write a dream story...your first awareness
   of dreams...your relationship to dreams, do
   you write them down? Your last dream, your
   association to its images...

e) Write a revelation of something Sacred...

Erato

Erato, translated as *lovely,* is the muse of erotic poetry, of awareness of love and its many expressions. The poet Fredrick Turner describes her as she who "... translates Eros from an external overmastering force into an internal skill of words and feeling." [131] It is her special gift to inspire the capacity for love as well as creative responses in its expression. Angeles Arrien describes Erato as the Muse "...who mediated between all forms of love and the human and spiritual experience of expressing love fully. She is often considered to be the emissary of Eros." [132] Arrien further imagines that an experience of authentic love is a blending of the four types of love that have been explored in Western philosophical traditions: *eros, libido, philia,* and *agape* or *caritas.* [133] She envisions Erato as the muse who balances these four types and creates the appropriate combination in each human experience of love. Sometimes an experience of love will be accented by *eros*, especially when there is a drive to create something original by bringing together two distinct entities and melding them into a unique new form. Other times love will be underscored with *libido*, with an emphasis on physical desire and sexuality. When the experience of friendship is the prominent feature, *philia* is emphasized. *Agape* or *caritas* is the kind of love which appears with transfigured desire, the realm in which the welfare of others and compassion for humanity are the primary concerns.

Erato reminds us of the power of love to witness, to heal, and to connect us with one another. The presence of love incites a yearning for knowledge, to know the Other more deeply, more completely. Erato insists we creatively convey our feelings, that we give expression to the beauty in which we find ourselves. It is she who appears as a third presence in the lover's dyad; both inspiring and bearing witness to those moments when the two catch each other's eyes, touch hands, kiss. Turner imagines her presence in such moments as "... delicate, so tactful, so civilized, that the triangle has a special frisson to it. ... perhaps she envies us our mortal love, the irreversibility of our erotic choice."[134] This kind of musing occurs in relationship, and is present in the attractions we feel and bonds we develop with significant others in our life. It is the awareness of beauty in the Other and our own capacity to appreciate it. As with Terpsichore and Euterpe, the body becomes the conduit of this muse's inspiration. Turner describes Erato's power:

> Erato has the special mission of showing us that if we would apprehend that beauty— which is really the whole meaning of life and the direct union with all of nature, and with nature's divine soul—then the best way of doing so is by the contemplation in sexual adoration of one's beloved. [135]

A memoir written under Erato's inspiration will bear witness to the loves of a person's life. It will understand that the telling of a life, the crafting of a memoir, *is* a kind of love story. To tell a life story requires compassion and respect for all that has led to the very need to write it. It is a profound act of self love, born out of myriad pains and pleasures. Erato gives the memoirist the courage to speak the truths of her experiences, reminding her that bearing witness is one way to demonstrate the power of love.

Erato may inspire tellings that include the initiations of first loves, first losses, moments of deep connection, of passion, of knowing an Other, of recognizing the mystery in human relationships, of sacred union. She is the muse who will ask a woman to draw recollections from her body, acknowledging the power and depth of sexual experiences that live in blood, bone, and muscle. Erato calls forth the stories of passion, tenderness, friendship, and connection to that-which-is-larger-than-ourselves. She shapes a text by insisting the writer craft the telling to match the tale, to draw from her heart the form that best fits the story. What follows is one of my own.

Flight of Mind

It is vacation. I am standing in the kitchen with my sister, helping unload groceries. The kids slam through the front door in a gale of shrieks common to cousins who see each other just once a year.

"So, did I tell you Richard said to say hi?"

She is stooping down, slinging cans of tomato soup into the cupboard next to the stove.

"His son goes to the same school as Alex. I see him at least once a week. His kid looks just like him. Coke bottle glasses and braces."

I fold the empty paper bag and lay it on the counter.

"Richard? I thought he had moved to Alaska. I can't believe he's still here."

"He married a girl from Hawaii, they have a house somewhere around Clackamas. In one of the new neighborhoods. He's been working as an air traffic controller for the Portland Airport."

"Air traffic controller? I wonder if he ever finished college. God, he was smart."

"Yeah, well some of us decided things aren't as bad here as they felt back then."

She glances at me and makes a face.

I draw a breath and let it go. Her point is that Us doesn't include me. I have been gone nearly twenty years, back for occasional vacations, small doses of Oregon evergreen and the scent of rain. Always returning to the sun baked central valley of California where the light is so intense, there is nowhere to hide from myself.

It is odd to make the trips, watch my sister's kids grow, see the few stray gray hairs at her temple, to recognize time passing at a distance. Still, there are moments I can be jolted backwards, a time warp triggered by the mention of a name. Richard. His face floats behind my eyes. Thick uneven hair, dark framed glasses, chipped front tooth. The dark mole on his cheek. How he always smelled of bark and leaves and summer.

I had just turned eighteen. My high school graduation only a few weeks before. I had gotten word from a small liberal Arts college that I had been accepted for the fall freshman class, and would have enough scholarship money and financial aid to make it possible. College. The brass ring. I would be the first one in my family. The weeks of July and August were filtering by in a curious haze of anxiety, anticipation, euphoria particular to the threshold of adulthood. If I could just hold on. My mother was burned out and on the perpetual edge of breakdown. There were five of us kids, me the oldest. One of my younger sisters was hell bent on doing whatever she wanted at the moment. Tension hung invisible ropes, at our every coming and going. It wasn't just my sister. She wasn't a bad kid, it was normal adolescent stuff, skipping classes, going to parties where everyone tried to get drunk as fast as they could before the cops showed up. Infractions which resulted in icy silence from our mother and sarcastic barbs from our stepfather. Since he worked late shift at the mill, we were mostly able to avoid him. Except for my two little brothers. They were still in junior high, not yet driving. Trapped. I remember their posture, stoop shouldered, heads ducked. They cowered.

I just wanted out.

It was a Monday. My mom had already left for the bank in Molalla. She had finished a nursing degree just before marrying for the second time, only to find a work place unsympathetic to a working mother with five kids. She was unable to find any day shift work at the local hospitals, settled for work at a convalescent center in order to be home by six in the evening. After two years of the horrors of working with old people with inadequate help in a ramshackle building, mom had relinquished her dream of being a nurse and went back to the bank. Steady hours that did not include weekend duty or calling families to convey news of deterioration or death. My grandmother had been in accounting for years, managing budgets and money. Numbers offered a certain predictability, they cooperated in columns, could be balanced at the end of the day, made no emotional demands. Numbers, it seemed, were imprinted in my mother's psyche. She had seen her own mother master them and support the family after her own father fell from a ladder and was unable to work for several years. Grandma toiled in a tiny office, for the sake of her girls. And as if history were repeating itself, Mom went back to totaling numbers for our sakes, so she could be home in the evenings. But part of her seemed to die. The best she got from the bank was its predictability, the worst was the constant reminder that she would never have the kind of career, the kind of choices, she had hoped for She watched other people's checks come through her window, watched them save their money, helped them fill out loan forms, watched them build houses, buy boats, send their kids off to college. Meanwhile, every penny she earned barely kept the mortgage paid. We were all used to buying our own school clothes, and meal times were large pots of whatever had been cheap that week. The truth was she was too exhausted to care any more.

The phone rang. It was Richard. He had been taking classes at the community college for the past year. We had a lot in common, mostly trying to figure out how to make it out of the backwoods where logging or farming were the two major career choices.

"How would you like to go to the beach today?"

"The beach?"

We lived outside of Oregon City, and while we were close to the river, the ocean was a good two and a half hour drive.

"Well, I guess so. Where are you planning to drive?"

"Not drive. Fly. I still need to log another couple hundred hours to make it to the next pilot's class. Remember, I've got my basic license."

Like I could have missed that. He had been working on getting his pilot's license for the past two years. While it had been his major obsession, he had yet to find a college course of study that could capture his long term dedication. He aced calculus, chemistry, all the physical science classes he ever took. His hero was Linus

Pauling. *He was the Nobel prize winner who had once lived in Beavercreek, our rural postal designation. Richard spoke his name with hushed reverence. Proof that even though we lived out in the middle of nowhere, great things were possible. You just had to have a dream. That, and money to pay for tuition.*

"Are you sure you know what you're doing? You aren't going to crash us anywhere are you?"

"Well, not on purpose. I'm good at this. Really. Besides, my instructor is giving me a deal on the plane rental for the afternoon, and I thought I'd share. So do you want to go?"

I was home by myself, except for Becky.

"Why not? I've been listening to talk about flying forever. I guess I'm ready to see how it works."

"Great. I can get the plane around eleven thirty. We'll leave from the Mulino airport. I have little brother duty today, you don't mind if he comes along do you?"

"Well no, but do you suppose there would be room for Becky too? If she finds out I flew to the beach for the afternoon and she didn't get to go I'll never hear the end of it."

"Not a problem. The plane has seats for four. So I'll be over around eleven O.K.?"

I hung up the phone.

Richard had been calling a lot during the past year. We had spent afternoons canoeing on the Clackamas River in Oregon City. Both of us lazy in the sun, while his little brother threw rocks at the shore and my little sister shrieked every time one splashed or the boat rocked. We went out to dinner once, another evening to an Olivia Newton John concert. I was beginning to notice sparks in his eyes. I thought we could just be friends, escape was my main preoccupation. I couldn't afford any detours.

"Hey Becky, want to go to the beach for the afternoon?"

I walked into our bedroom.

"Becky?"

She was sprawled out on the bed staring at the ceiling.

"There is nothing to do around here. Nothing. I am so bored."

"Did you hear what I said? That was Richard. He's got a rental plane for the afternoon and wants to log some hours. He invited us to come. So do you want to go?"

"He knows how to fly? Are you sure?"

She was sitting up now.

"Yeah, he's finished all his instrument tests and all of his supervised flights. He's had his license for the past couple of months. Besides, he has to take his little brother with him, so it's not like a date or anything."

She rolled her eyes.

"Right. He likes you, you idiot."

"Come on. You don't want to be stuck here all by yourself this afternoon do you?"

She rolled off the bed.

"Count me in, but you have to promise I won't have to watch any kissy face stuff." I threw a pillow at her head.

The day was clear and sunny. A few high clouds, but nowhere near full enough to threaten rain. Richard had picked up the keys from the office. We stood at the edge of the field staring at the gap toothed rows of tiny airplanes. There couldn't have been more than thirty planes parked in the entire field, some parked under makeshift hangers, some parked out in open air on the grass. The checkered windsock that hung near the end where we stood was faded and frayed. There was just enough flat dirt at right angles to convince an onlooker that yes, this really was an airport. A country sort of one anyway.

"Got the paperwork taken care of. Had to file a flight plan. Estimate our return time. You guys ready?"

He waved us out to the field, toward a dusty blue four-seater. The closer we got, the more I realized it looked like the outside of an aluminum trailer, bolts, seams, worn color.

"You've been up in this one a lot, right?"

"Hey, she may not look like much but she is a sturdy as they come."

He thumped the side by the door for emphasis. It twanged like an empty barrel. I was not reassured.

He reached up to unlatch the door. It swung open easily.

"Come on. Once you look inside you'll feel better."

Becky and John scrambled in first.

"Wow, this is so cool! I want to sit on this side." The rear seats were stacked tight, each with a window the size of a dinner plate.

I climbed in and sat down. Not much different than a passenger seat in a car really. Except for all the dials, and the unmistakable outline of wings and propellers which hovered on the edge of vision.

Richard climbed up and sat down.

"So what do you think, do you trust me?"

His hands were already making adjustments to the various gages, eyes scanning the windows. I never even blinked.

"I'm ready if you are."

We finished putting away groceries, feed the kids, and finally sit down at the kitchen table. I pick at the leftover sandwich crusts. Kris is in the stage where crusts are not in her repertoire.

"Can you believe we really did that? Flying to the beach for an afternoon? Not even calling Mom?"

We both shake our heads, laughing at the memory, our sheer willful youth.

"If my kids ever did anything like that without telling me first I'd freak. Honest to God, freak."

"They won't."

Right, I think. Like we know this. Like we can tell ourselves stories and convince ourselves that we have already paid the price, and so now our kids won't have to.

"Right, they're our kids, they'd tell us."

I have turned the pieces of that afternoon so many times. Looking for a tiny sliver of myself at eighteen, a piece I might have missed. I've never found it. Not a glimmer. The one marked Caution. Not even a vague inkling that I should have let anyone else know where we had gone, what we planned to do. I just said yes, and the afternoon unfolded. Unfolded with ease common to deep grace. Like breath, like scent, like music.

We took off, gliding over the patchwork of farmland and fir trees.

"Look down there, that's the highway we drive to the coast. Over there, do you see the river?"

The water of the Willamette River sparkled below us, a thin silver ribbon, winding through dark and light patches of green.

We could see Mount Hood to one side. We floated over farmland and then the city of McMinnville. Rooftops clustered more densely, then spread out again. We could make out the river even as it emptied into the ocean, broad, grey and blue. It didn't take long at all, maybe forty-five minutes. One moment we had been back at the ramshackle Mulino Airport, the next, we were climbing down a retaining wall, and running along packed sand. Not far from Lincoln City, salt water taffy, and tide pools. The sun was out, and the sky was blue. A rare combination for the Oregon beach. The wind gusted, the waves were bottle glass green. We walked along the beach until clouds covered the sun, and the water turned grey. Wet sand worked its way into the seams of my clothes, crunched between my teeth, settled into my hairline. We had taken off our shoes, searched the line of the tide for shells and pieces of driftwood. I had a handful of small blue mussel shells, one whole one, perfectly hinged, the rest single halves, worn smooth. My hair was stiff with salty grit.

"Time we were heading back?"

Richard waved down Becky and John, both intent on writing their names into the sand with sticks of driftwood. The water lapped over their efforts. They chased the water out, stomping and splashing, as the tide retreated.

"Come on you guys, I promised I'd have the plane back by five."

My youngest daughter comes in to show me her latest crayon rendition of the family.

"This is you and this is Daddy, and here is me." It is red and blue and loopy. All of the faces have huge smiles.

I give her a hug, and she flits off to another activity, comprehensible only to her five-year-old mind. Our butterfly.

I think what a path she has traveled to arrive here in our midst. With me as her mother and David her father. I am grateful she waited for us, came when our relationship had melded into something solid. I can't help but realize she wouldn't have come had I decided to settle down with a different person. A different man. I am overcome with emotion, water smarts up in my eyes, blurs my vision. I am grateful for my life.

    The day came for me to report to the dorms. I don't remember my mother making the trip, only Richard. Packing the back seat of his beat up car with my bedding, two suitcases, a few boxes of books, and my prize typewriter. Being euphoric and melancholy all at once. Waving good bye to my sisters, hugging my brothers, watching the country roads fade behind us. Wondering for the ten millionth time if this was really me, if any of this was real.

    My room was on the second floor in a complex named Forrest. Five buildings arranged around a courtyard, surrounded by trees and azaleas. We lugged all my stuff up the stairs, groaning and joking about bricks in the boxes. I was in a room at the end of the hall with three other girls, none of whom I knew. Suddenly I was scared of all the unknowns.

    I was standing in the middle of the dorm room with all my worldly possessions, a small pile compared to the trunks and suitcases I had glimpsed in other rooms.

    "You all right?"

    I sat down on top of my biggest suitcase, the plaid one with the duct tape holding a split in the fabric.

    "I guess so."

    "Look, you'll be fine. This place is great. It's what you've always wanted."

    I looked at him standing in the door way, his face trying to smile. I got up and hugged him hard, felt the muscles in his torso tighten, smelled summer in the skin along his neck.

    We promised to call each other, to keep in touch. He was trying to decide whether or not Oregon State would be a good transfer choice, whether or not he would be able to scrape together enough money to get himself through. I waved to him from the dorm window until his car followed the curve of the road and was gone. I closed my eyes and hoped hard for the best. For both of us.

    It is twilight. My sister and I are sitting outside on the deck, the view is beautiful. A deeply wooded slope that breaks open onto the valley floor, dotted with city lights that stretch to the horizon. We can even see the Fremont Bridge, its single arch a perfect symmetry. The air is sweet with smells of bark, fir trees, damp even when it's not raining.

We sip our wine, and I ache from sleeping in a bed that's not my own. The kids have settled down with compromises, flashlights under blanket tents, promises to whisper.

"Do you ever wonder what your life would have been like if you had married someone else?"

Her eyes never shift from the horizon.

"Every day."

Our husbands are both inside, slouched back on the couch, sports channel flickering across their faces. I can see Dave's profile, see the images from the TV screen reflected off his glasses.

"I don't mean I'm sorry, but things could have turned out a hundred different ways..."

"What's done is done. Things could be worse."

This is my sister's stock answer to just about anything that refers to our past. I have learned not to pursue these topics, as we see things differently.

She rises to go inside, I stay and let the twinkle of the lights pull me into more flights of reverie, remembering and remembering.

I met Dave my freshman year, on a Jesus retreat. I had decided this was a safe group to hang out with. New Testament Christianity had an immediacy that was reassuring, the communal way of life appealed to my social sensibilities. He had already graduated with a degree in English, and was one of the study group leaders for the weekend. His wire rim glasses framed large blue eyes, and his hair was gold. Sort of John Denver. I had been intrigued, but didn't really think he even noticed me. After all his world was concerned with making a living. He was watching and wondering as his friends begin to marry off in tidy pairs. Still, I remember thinking he was awfully cute. And serious about spiritual things. I admired that. Was I ever shocked to meet him coming down my dorm stairs a month later. By Valentine's Day we had spent several evenings together, and then he sent me a red rose along with an e.e. cummings poem. My plan to remain unencumbered by a serious relationship went dead in the water. We went out to eat, to a movie, Rocky, and then for a drive through Portland to watch the lights twinkle off the water. I had been certain city lights couldn't hold a candle to Silvercreek Falls or Mt. Hood. He was a city boy determined to prove me wrong.

Sometime toward the end of spring semester, I came into my dorm room to find several messages from Richard on my desk. He would be in Portland Friday night and wanted to stop by. I had already made vague plans to spend the evening with Dave. I had a sinking feeling. How could I explain to either of them. I knew already how it felt to have the blood pound in my ears, warm creeping up my arms, settle in my chest. I hoped I wouldn't have to hurt Richard's feelings, but I already knew it was too late for that.

"Hey, you are awfully quiet."
My sister comes outside and sits down.
"Yeah. Well. Portland is so pretty from here."
"Distance hides the grit. From a lot of things."
"That's why you think I didn't hang around?"
She laughs. "You tell me. You're the one who comes here for vacation every year."
I groan. I wasn't the one who thought city lights were so romantic twenty years ago, but once I had been convinced, it hadn't been my idea to leave. Graduate school had called, and scholarships didn't grow on trees. My sister still didn't understand why we left.
"Life is funny."
I finish my wine and go in to check on the kids. They have been so quiet, and I find them sleeping soundly, a tangle of arms, legs, pillows, and stuffed animals twisted in the center of the living room floor. Skin like rose petals. Innocent.

The house is dark. I rummage in my suitcase for my night shirt and fall asleep next to David. In my dreams I am flying back home with Richard, the sun is setting behind us. The sky is gold and peach and rose. The whole of our little world is laid out below, fir trees, berry fields, tiny two-lane country roads that wind like kite tails. Mount Hood stands perfect guardian, pure white peak against blue dusk. In the distance on the other side, we can make out Three Sisters, a trio bright as truth. They shine like diamonds in the last of the sun light.

I can see Richard's profile as he flies. The light casts shadows in front of us. I can see the river below reflected on the surface of his glasses. It's as if I am seeing what he is seeing by observing the reflection off his lenses. There are farms, rivers, creeks, blackberry bramble, broken fences. I see the twinkling lights of small cities start to flicker on, I see clumps of houses spread farther and farther apart. Until I see my own. I do not want to land. I want to keep flying, to stay aloft and notice how seamless all the places really are. Up there the view is magic, unbroken. But we land. The runway is grassy, and we bump along the surface until the engine slows to a dull roar.

I am waving goodbye to Richard. Tears are streaming down my cheeks, down his.

He turns and raises his hand one last time.

"Thank you, Thank you."

I raise my arms, lift off the ground, I am flying. I push up into the cool night air, drink the starlight.

I can see the river, winding silver ribbon in the moonlight, see it all the way to the ocean. I am free. There is a burning in my chest, a star has formed, and light streams out. I fly on and on.

I wonder if Richard can see me.

I wake the next morning, my face wet, my heart full. Grateful for memory, for flight.

Erato Exercises:

a) write a story of a 'first' love

b) Write a story of 'brotherly-sisterly' love

c) Write a story of 'sensual' love

d) Write an experience of 'unconditional' love...

e) Who were 'teachers of your heart'? How would you describe their lessons to you? How are those lessons present in your life today?

f) What is your favorite love story/ romantic movie? How does this story parallel (or not!) your own experience of love?

g) Tristine Rainer, author of *Your Life as Story*, suggests that, it memoir as well as fiction, motivation must be a constant element: "The character [you] should have a clear desire line. It can bend, it can turn unexpectedly, but it should not break. It should be intense and continuous. As soon as one need is met, another appears."

Map out your own 'desire' line on a piece of paper. Look at the places where it changes from desire for a relationship to desire for a particular relationship, then to desiring what comes next.... The complications of formal commitment, or not (!) Jot down the incidents that illustrate the various stages of desire as they are challenged by conflicting needs or circumstances.

h) Engage your sense of scent. Think about the smells you associate with a loved one. Let the memory of this fragrance inspire you to write. Make a list of twenty-five smells—pleasant and unpleasant, natural and industrial. Choose one as a writing catalyst and let it trigger images, thoughts, and feelings. Go into your kitchen and smell some spices. Visit the bathroom and open some jars.

These reflections on how each of the Muses is related to a particular form of memoir writing shows how Mnemosyne offers myriad possibilities for the shaping of a text. Her daughters the Muses each offer unique inflections for the various sorts of forms a text can take. While each offers a distinct style in crafting a memoir, each calls the others to mind as a metonymy. They are, after all, their mother's daughters, intent on drawing together spirit and matter, on creating wholeness. Dupree expresses it thus, "The Muses are, finally, the necessarily different notes of the one melody, at once symphonic and heterophonic. To make music, they need one another." [136]

The Greek notion of memory was different from ours today. In Greek culture, all artwork was imagined as being mid-wifed by the Muses. Each representation was not understood as something brand new out of the artist's psyche, but rather an incarnation of an archaic Memory. Within this imaginal framework, a mortal's task was to re-member a myth that already existed implicitly in the culture and then deliver it to the larger collective with the recognition that such creations are simply Memory re-membering Herself. Each of the Muses, with her unique style of inspiration and influence on the shaping of a text, ultimately leads back to grandmother Gaia, with each part carrying the whole, much like a hologram. Philosopher Kathleen Dean Moore captures this sentiment succinctly:

> It's our memories that make us who we are....Every time I notice something, every time something strikes me as important enough to store away in my memory, I add another piece to who I am. These memories and sense impressions of the landscape are the very substance of my self. In this way I am–at the core of my being–made of the earth.[137]

Chapter Five:
Memoir and Healing

The only way through pain... is to absorb, probe, understand exactly what it is and what it means. To close the door on pain is to miss the chance for growth... Nothing that happens to us, even the most terrible shock, is unusable, and everything has somehow to be built into the fabric of the personality.— May Sarton138

Writing testimony, to be sure, means that we tell our stories. But it also means that we no longer allow ourselves to be silenced or allow others to speak for our experience. Writing to heal, then, and making that writing public, as I see it, is the most important emotional, psychological, artistic, and political project of our time.—Louise DeSalvo139

Let's considers the question: "Why do I choose to write memoir?" In thinking about the Bloom and Lahey Venn diagram, *use* is the area where content and form are placed into action, the place where the goals of the speaker are considered. It is also where one considers the influence of context, the experiences which figure into how a person comes to understand and choose among possible forms of language for specific purposes.[140] I would like to explore the idea of 'use' more specifically as a way of healing from trauma or painful experiences. This trajectory is in keeping with Mnemosyne since she was the daughter who witnessed the trauma of her own mother. Mnemosyne's birthing of the Muses underscores her commitment to express all the facets of personal story: grief, sorrow, joy, love, body, breath, reverie, and humor. The memoirist follows Mnemosyne's imaginal lineage in crafting all memoir, and most especially those that recount painful events. I consider memoir writing an opportunity for 'textual healing,' a phrase coined by Farrah Jasmin Griffiths, and inspired by Marvin Gaye's pop lyrics *Sexual Healing.*[141]

The year of my eleventh birthday, my parents divorced and my mother remarried a month later. To a pedophile. I wouldn't learn that word until years later, and to this day, it sounds too kind to my ears. How could such evil behavior be given a name that meant something as innocent sounding as 'child lover'? He was a seducer and serial molester; when he had finished with his own children, he found a woman, my mother, with five more. He started with me. No one in my family seemed to notice. There was no one to tell, not even my teachers at school. I lived in terror that I would be found out and that we would all be sent to foster care. I would not speak of it until I moved away and made friends who could listen and not recoil in horror when I finally spoke the stories aloud. Healing came through words, and eventually, through writing. Placing events on paper gave me courage and helped me gradually come to understand the context which created the painful and difficult circumstances of my family of origin.

I grew to embrace my own story, and writing helped me imagine my motherline and understand how their injuries led to their own silencing. Memoir writing has led me to a place where my former work as a therapist with children and language disorders left off. I am still a 'worker in story,' but I have moved into the realm of metaphor. I still find the power of language in the structuring of narratives, though now I have also found the way to pick up what were once broken and dangerous pieces of memory and re-member in such a way that the story can be passed on. The memories no longer make me bleed when I run my fingers along their edge.

. . . .

I felt caught in time distortions.
Images of my mother and Art welled up and threatened to swallow me
whole. My mind was bending in slow broad waves, I felt the tension being
stretched and pulled into hideous distortions of myself, unable to find a

place where truth was certain, a place where I could trust the reflection. Summer was on its way, and now Mom was making plans with Art. I heard them talking in the kitchen after we had gone to bed. Talking about where they would live, how they would meld two families. I couldn't believe it was true. How could he, how could she? I was sure I would be damned to Hell for all that had happened. Adultery. That was the word I heard in church. Adultery. Sex without marriage was Adultery. He said he'd take care of me and I had believed him. I had believed him. I thought I was the one he would take away to a New Life. I didn't know what to think of my Mother. How could she choose him? There had been other men in our house since Dad had left. I'd seen them kiss her in the living room when they thought we weren't around. The aura of sex around our house was palpable. How could she marry him? Why couldn't she just live without any of them? Why couldn't I? I was unprepared for the enormity of all that was sweeping through me and over me. I was about to drown.

"Your mother and I are going to be married."

I was standing in the kitchen in his run down house. It was the morning. I don't know where the others were, but we were alone. I was sick. I stood at the sink, retching. He stood off by the table. "It had to come to this. I am 27 years older than you, it can't work. What am I supposed to do, run away with you? We'd never get very far, and then I'd be arrested for kidnapping a child."

A child. The word slapped me in the face, with such a force my knees buckled. A child.

I saw the sun on his face. His thick glasses. The bags under his squinty eyes. The stubble on his skin had gray spikes in it. He was wearing a worn t-shirt and cotton work pants. His teeth were yellow from smoking. I thought I'd loved him.

"You know your mother would never understand this. You know what this would do to her. You don't want to see her go to Damasch do you?" He took steps closer, trying to get near, to put his hand on my shoulder. It was too late for comfort. I was numb, though I could feel animal rage seeping into my throat, I could not give it voice. Not yet.

My mother, my mother. Of course. She was the only thing that could stop me dead in my tracks. Damasch was the state mental hospital. My mother had hurled the name around the walls at home whenever her stress level got too high and she was near dissolution. If she were to go, we would surely end up county foster homes. I'd

114

*seen what had happened to a boy in my class in school when his
mother cracked up. We would be split up, never see each other again,
have the word "abandoned" branded on our foreheads for life. He
knew how much fear those words conjured. He pressed on.*

"You don't want her to go to Damasch do you?"

His words torn like blades. I swallowed what tasted like blood.

*"Remember I'm the adult, you are the child. You're going to
start acting like it."*

He accented the a in adult. Aaadult.

Trauma

Psychiatrist Judith Lewis Herman describes the effect of
traumatic events as those that "shatter the construction of the self
that is formed and sustained in relation to others"; further, it can
"cast the victim into a state of existential crisis."[142] A trauma is an
overwhelming experience that shocks the psyche, a shock that is too
big to be integrated at the moment it is experienced. Cathy Caruth
further describes how a person's pathology, her or his response to
trauma, cannot be defined by the event itself, which may or may
not be catastrophic, and might not traumatize each person equally;
nor can it be understood only as a distortion of an event, which
haunts because of the distorting personal significances attached.[143]
Caruth observes further how the pathology consists "...solely in the
structure of its experience or reception: the event is not assimilated
or experienced fully at the time, but only belatedly, in its repeated
possession of the one who experiences it. To be traumatized is
precisely to be possessed by an image or event." [144]

Possession by such an event or image has come to be understood
in contemporary psychological parlance as Post Traumatic Stress
Disorder, or PTSD. Caruth summarizes current descriptions of this
diagnosis as "a response, sometimes delayed, to an overwhelming
event or events... [and] takes the form of repeated intrusive
hallucinations, dreams, thoughts, or behaviors stemming from the
event. "[145] Characteristics include both psychic numbing, initially
from the event, and hyper-arousal and avoidance of stimuli, which
recall the initial wounding. After-effects can manifest in dangerous
behaviors which are an attempt to ease profound psychic pain. There

is little doubt that traumatic events precipitate a fragmentation of the image of the 'integrated' person.

Herman classifies the collection of symptoms of post traumatic stress disorder as: a state of persistent expectation of danger; constriction at the moment of impact; and the numbing response of surrender. Memories of traumatic events are obtrusive and haunting, and become stored in the brain with an adrenaline rush paired with the biological response to danger. As a result, traumatic impact is "...not encoded like ordinary moments of adults in verbal, linear narrative." [146] Instead they are imprinted in the neurological system in the form of vivid images and feelings. As untended injuries, these traumatic memories do not progress, but remain static and repetitious, constantly present at the periphery of consciousness. Recent brain research by Bessel van der Kolk and Daniel Schacter indicate that traumatic memories are not processed in the cerebral cortex but in the more primitive area of the amygdala. These researchers postulate that the release of stress-related hormones are most likely responsible for the power and persistence of the traumatic experiences.[147]

Caruth notes how the traumatic scene/thought is not possessed knowledge, but itself possesses the individual. She further observes a peculiar paradox, "...that in trauma the greatest confrontation with reality may also occur as an absolute numbing to it, that immediacy, paradoxically enough, may take the form of belated-ness."[148] It is as if a massive trauma leaves a psychic hole; that its very shock precludes the person's ability to register it.[149] Laub describes this phenomenon as a "collapse of witnessing," a characteristic common to traumatic experiences. [150] Caruth observes that to fully witness a traumatic event is to do so at the expense of witnessing one's own self. [151] As a result, a gap is created at the expense of knowledge and memory. "The force of the experience would appear to arise precisely .... in the collapse of its understanding." [152] The experience is beyond the person's capacity to process it; she is, in effect, not fully present at the moment of impact. Emily Dickinson describes such an experience of trauma in the following poem:

There is a pain—so utter—

    It swallows substance up—
    Then covers the Abyss with Trance—

So Memory can step
Around—across—upon it—
As one within a Swoon—
Goes safely— where an open eye—
Would drop him— Bone by Bone. [153]

The abyss of which Dickinson writes is that very collapse described by Laub. It holds an event which so terrifies a person, that entering it would result in one's total psychic annihilation. Trauma is paradoxical in that it

> ...is not experienced as a mere repression or defense, but as a temporal delay that carries the individual beyond the shock of the first moment. The trauma is a repeated suffering of the event, but also a continual leaving of its site.... by carrying [the] impossibility of knowing out of the empirical event itself, trauma opens up and challenges us to a new kind of listening, the witnessing, precisely, of impossibility. [154]

Perhaps revisiting trauma can be tolerated more easily in the creation of text; one can put it down for a moment, choose which details and how many to include for a specific scene. The writing of memoir, particularly of a memoir focused on a traumatic experience, can still address the need to pass out of the isolation imposed by the event, can still set in motion the awareness of what a survivor of a particular trauma has to say, can still offer medicine to the larger culture. Memoir offers the writer an opportunity to witness both the suffering of a traumatic event and to leave the site of that suffering. It offers the survivor of trauma an increase in flexibility; one can create multiple vantage points in a text, recognizing a text can always be revised. Caruth poetically suggests that "...trauma itself may provide the very link between cultures: not a simple understanding of the pasts of others but rather, within the traumas of contemporary history, as our ability to listen through the departures we have all taken from ourselves." [155] Recitation of trauma in the form of memoir holds the potential for recognizing both multiple and universal frames of experience, as well as returning to and departing from traumatic life experiences.

Pioneers in the field of psychiatry including Jean-Martin Charcot, Pierre Janet and William James were all interested in the flexibility of the mind as well as problematic memories which seemed to keep some patients from engaging in life. Pierre Janet developed a comprehensive formulation on the effects of traumatic memories on consciousness. He proposed that actual memories may form the nucleus of psychopathology and continue to exert their influence by means of the process of dissociation.[156] According to Henri Ellenberger, Janet was the first to use the term "subconscious" for the collection of automatically stored memories that form the map that subsequently guides interaction with the environment.[157] Janet maintained that healthy psychological functioning depended on the proper operation of the memory system, which consists of a unified memory of all psychological facets related to particular experiences; sensations, emotions, thoughts, action.[158]

Janet noted specific differences between ordinary narrative memory and traumatic memory. Traumatic memory has no social component; it's not addressed to anyone; the person doesn't respond to anyone; it is a solitary recollection. By contrast, narrative memory serves a social function and is a means of appealing for help or making connections. Further, traumatic memory can be evoked under particular situations, especially those reminiscent of the original trauma in sensory content; sight, sound, touch, smell, taste. Traumatic memory may also require an affective and motoric repetition of the original trauma. Ordinary narrative memory is able to be stored in language, retrieved in a time efficient manner, used in an adaptable manner, depending on the social circumstances.

Janet believed it was the intensity of emotional experiences that caused a lack of proper integration into the memory system and resulted in both dissociation and the formation of traumatic memories. He proposed that these traumatic memories were new cores of consciousness and called them "subconscious fixed ideas." While such ideas were under the surface of conscious awareness, Ellenberger points out that Janet felt they persist in influencing current behavior, affect states, and perceptions.[159] Furthermore, such "subconscious fixed ideas" are simultaneously both cause and effect of mental difficulties. Janet was one of the first to note that those seeking psychiatric care often display disassociative behavior: they react inappropriately to stress, behave automatically in ways that correspond to the fragmented re-experience of the original trauma. [160] Janet used the word "attached," while Freud preferred the term "fixated" to describe what such individuals experienced. Unable to understand the source of their terror, they are unable to assimilate subsequent experiences. Janet's idea of the subconscious as containing affectively-charged material encoded in altered states of awareness influenced much of what Freud wrote in the years between 1892 and 1896. [161] He also followed Janet's idea of attachment to trauma and proposed that the compulsion to repeat the trauma is a function of repression. Freud went on to claim that if a person does not remember, he is likely to act out.

Since this early work on memory and trauma, contemporary neuro-psychology has continued to explore the topic. All memories are malleable by constant re-working, recasting, reorganizing, yet traumatic memories become fixed and not altered by time's passing or subsequent life events. [162] One neurological explanation for the "fixedness" of traumatic memories concerns myelinization; the maturation of nerve sheaths in the brain. Developmentally the brain is quite plastic until myelinization, but each part of the brain has its own schedule; thus, the whole process is not complete until the end of puberty. Dutch researcher Bessel Van der Kolk posits that if a trauma is experienced prior to the completion of the brain's "hard wiring", the information can't be integrated into the central nervous system. He further posits that a traumatic experience can be so overwhelming that it cannot be processed on a linguistic level, and because of this failure to sort the memory into words or symbols, it may be organized at a somatosensory or iconic level as somatic sensations, re-enactments, nightmares, flashbacks. Information which is stored at the iconic level must be retrieved differently; words alone can't pull it out. Analyst Marion Woodman's work with body memory presents the idea that women carry their traumas in their very bones, muscles, organs and that it takes much work to translate these somatic images into a conscious narrative which can then be worked and re-storied. [163] There has been extensive research in the past twenty-five years investigating the relationship of neurological and physiological underpinnings of response to trauma. While the precise relationship between trauma and body memory is still a subject of much debate, psychotherapist B. Rothschild asserts, "When healing trauma, it is crucial to give attention to both body and mind; you can't have one without the other."[164]

Traumatic experiences are encoded in memory in ways which cannot be accessed by language alone, and as Janet pointed out in his early work, patients needed to be brought back to the state in which the memory was first encoded in order that the dissociated memory can then be integrated into current frames of meaning. As van der Kolk describes them, "Traumatic memories are the un-assimilated scraps of overwhelming experiences, which need to be integrated with existing mental schemes and be transformed into narrative language."[165] The potential of recovery from previously debilitating after-effects is the goal of placing the event into narrative. The individual no longer suffers flashbacks, nightmares, or self destructive impulses, but now has the ability to tell the story, thereby enabling one to "... look back on what happened; he has given it a place in his life history, his autobiography. " [166]

Trauma and Creativity

As Mnemosyne is an imaginal template for writing memoir, it is important to revisit her experience of trauma. Her story suggests an image of trauma that results from masculine physical assault and subsequent control of the feminine. Hesiod's recitation of Mnemosyne's birth describes her as one of the Titan children whom her father, Ouranos, would not allow to be born. Mnemosyne then arrives not only to witness her mother's agony, but also experiences her own painful and claustrophobic beginnings. She becomes one of the Greeks' mythological figures who relates trauma to creative expression. Because she has been both observer and recipient of trauma, she is driven to create myriad forms for expression of such stories as evidenced by her own birthing of the nine Muses. Such prolific creativity in the artist has been observed by psychologist Andrew Brink who attributes exceptional levels of productivity to some earlier damage/trauma/pain. He notes that negative experiences are often the impetus behind the drive toward righting [writing], what went wrong early on in the writer's life.[167] Mnemosyne is a figure who understands the trauma of feminine body experience, one who will not forget, and one who inspires many inflections of recollection.

Writing memoir becomes one creative means of coping with trauma. Describing the details of one's life, making a narrative which speaks out, bears witness and causes the reader to consider his/her own relationships and experiences in light of this particular telling. The memoirist who chooses to re-tell traumatic experiences activates a process of cultural change, beginning with herself. It simultaneously creates both intimacy and distance with the story which presents itself. It is not difficult to see how a memoirist can provide a particular window on the topic of trauma in our culture. Alice Sebold's memoir, *Lucky,* is one such example of bringing female sexual violence into plain view. Written in 1999, Sebold recounts the story of her rape as an eighteen-year-old college freshman, and the aftermath of confronting and prosecuting the man responsible. She begins with an extremely graphic recounting of the event, excruciating in its recitation of the particulars of the assault. She concludes the scene with the line, "My life was over; my life had just begun." [168] By beginning her memoir with such a segment, she conveys the disorienting nature of trauma, how it arrives suddenly and without preparation, simulating the overwhelming shock of the experience. Sebold describes how her world and relationships with others was irrevocably altered post-rape. Once she tells her story to another person, she is never the same in his or her eyes. Rape brings myriad associations in its wake, and she describes feeling other people's embarrassment and self consciousness.

The aftermath of the rape spins her into a new social subculture, that of rape survivor. She recounts seeing her rapist on the street a few months later, reporting him to the police, securing his arrest, and the long process of going to trial. Sebold's unflinching honesty grounds this telling of a common female trauma in such a way that the reader is forever changed. She does not end her story at the conclusion of the trial, but also lays bare the rape of her best friend who is assaulted in what looks like "pay back" for Sebold's legal pursuit against the man who raped her. The best friend is unable to bring charges against her aggressor and ultimately steps away from

Sebold's friendship. Sebold faces more bitter after-effects of rape in her personal relationships, realizing how rape can also alienate survivors from each other.

Such a memoir has the effect of drawing the culture's attention to dark places, to its assumptions about sexuality and violence and how a woman survives such events. It draws a stark picture; this is how a rape happens to a young woman in contemporary America, this is how it looks, this is how it feels. Not only does such a memoir help the survivor come to terms with her experience of rape trauma and its aftermath, it also forces the reader to consider his/her own culpability in the cultural conversation on sexual violence. It functions as a creative means of revolution, challenging the culture's comfort level and calling for participation in the process of social change, one reader at a time.

Textual Healing: Healing the self

The Greek story of Mnemosyne conveys the trauma surrounding her birth: her feelings of anguish at her mother's pain from forbidden labor contractions and her experience of not being allowed to be born in a timely manner. Upon emerging from her mother's body, she assumes her role as the figure who will not forget such horror, the figure for whom the body becomes a repository of lived experiences, particularly those which are traumatic. She is the figure who takes up broken pieces of experience and places them in narrative, poetry, dance, and song. Because she is a daughter of Gaia, she inherits the quality of generativity. She evokes life from terrible wounds, no matter how ragged the edges. Because of her impulse to draw pieces together, Mnemosyne can be imagined as one of the first healers in the genealogies of Greek mythology. Webster's dictionary defines the verb "heal" as ' to make sound or whole, as in a wound, to restore to health, to cause an undesirable condition to be overcome, to mend, to restore to original purity or integrity.' I imagine Mnemosyne as the daughter of Gaia who is intent on bringing together broken pieces, of restoring wholeness to a life through re-membering a trauma. Indeed, the call toward narrative coherence, toward crafting a sense of wholeness seems to be a hallmark of contemporary memoir.

Louise DeSalvo affirms the connection between writing and the move toward restoring a sense of wholeness about the events of one's life. "Ultimately, then, writing about difficulties enables us to discover the wholeness of things, the connectedness of human experience. We understand that our greatest shocks do not separate us from human kind. Instead, through expressing ourselves, we establish our connection with others and with the world." [169]

Because Mnemosyne offers multiple ways of recalling an event, she introduces the quality of flexibility in dealing with traumatic events. It is her particular gift of flexibility which offers potential healing of a traumatic memory. "Memory is everything. Once flexibility is introduced, the traumatic memory starts losing its power over current experience. By imagining [these] alternative scenarios, many [writers] are able to soften the intrusive power of the original, unmitigated horror." [170] One such example comes from Mark Doty's memoir Heaven's Coast, in which he observes, "What is healing but a shift in perspective?" [171] Doty chronicles the story of his partner's life and death with AIDS, and gives voice to how his own healing is ongoing as he reconstructs the events of his life through the process of writing.

Writing personal narratives has helped many heal from the effects of loss, grief, personal tragedy by providing a vehicle which facilitates new ways of coping with life's challenges. Writer Louise DeSalvo recognizes the value of trauma, since traumatic experiences "… realign the essential nature of our being," explaining how trauma creates new perspectives. She poses an important question; "What if writing were a simple, significant, yet necessary way to achieve spiritual, emotional, and psychic wholeness? To synthesize thought and feeling, to understand how feeling relates to the events in our lives and vice versa?"[172] To which I would make another extension: What if writing has been an archetypal mode of healing since Hesiod first recorded the *Theogony*? One can imagine Mnemosyne standing behind the impulse to craft a memoir: to join the elements of thought, emotion, and body experience, elements made disparate by trauma.

In 1985 Suzette Henke delivered a paper at the MLA convention in Chicago on a tentative paradigm for what she termed "scripto-therapy"— the process of writing out and writing through traumatic experience in the mode of therapeutic re-enactment. She observes that "...if one accepts the basic premise of Freud's talking cure, a psycho-analytic working through of repressed memories brought to the surface and abreacted through the use of language and free association," then it is perhaps possible that the power of healing resides not in the therapist but in the experience of the "re-memory" and reenactment of such memories.[173] DeSalvo agrees with this assessment. "Through writing, we revisit our past and review and revise it. What we thought happened, what we believe happened, shifts and changes as we discover deeper and more complex truths. It isn't that we use our writing to deny what we experienced. Rather, we use it to shift our perspective."[174] Such observations bring to mind the metaphor of the kaleidoscope; the memoir itself becomes the instrument by which we are able to shift perspective on events we live through. DeSalvo imagines the healing properties of memoir come from its very capacity to move to new perspectives, to come to a way of telling one's life story in a manner that is "... marked by acceptance, authenticity, depth, serenity, and wisdom, that is the hallmark of genuine healing."[175] DeSalvo offers the analogy of writing as "fixer"; referencing the chemicals used in photography as a means of stabilizing an image. She imagines writing as a way to stabilize one's impressions of particular events, holding them "fixed" long enough to reflect and associate new meanings. She also proposes "fixing" as a double entendre for healing; it is a way of mending what was broken, of healing the injured parts of one's self.

Henke observes that in any autobiographical text, the writer assumes the roles of both analyst and analysand. Through the writing process the writer theoretically restores a sense of agency to the previously fragmented self, now recast as the protagonist of her own life story. She notes that if the repetitious cycle of PTSD is to be broken, the person must reenact the trauma with the details: physical, sensory, psychological, and emotional. She asserts that the object of psychotherapy and scripto-therapy is the same: to reassemble the pieces of the trauma and translate them into a coherent verbal account. Psychiatrist Judith Lewis Herman notes clinical outcomes for PTSD are positively influenced with the "action of telling a story."[176] She describes the construction of a narrative account of trauma as means for transforming the traumatic memory as well as a way of alleviating many of the symptoms of PTSD. Upon reviewing clinical outcomes which emphasize the construction of narratives she concludes: "The physio-neurosis induced by terror can apparently be reversed through the use of words." [177] Herman observes that the act of articulating/writing can transform a traumatic experience into a testimony, into a "ritual of healing." [178] Writing becomes the action that creates the medicine the injured psyche requires. It provides both the container and content that needs to be constructed to restore a sense of wholeness to the self. Henke points out the term *narrative recovery* pivots on the double entendre that evokes both the recovery of past experience through narrative construction as well as the psychological reintegration of the trauma survivor. [179] Writing memoir can be a form of restitution, a way of righting a wrong that has been done to you.

In summary, those of us who chose to write through our trauma may discover potential healing from engaging such a process. Alice Walker believes "It is, in the end, the saving of lives that we writers are about... We do it because we care... We care because we know this: *the life we save is our own.*" [180] Memoir writing has the potential to work as a means of redemption/salvation, a means for creatively redirecting self destructive impulses, a means of healing an injured self, a means of returning one to meanngful community participation.

For further reflection on healing and writing exercises:

James Pennebaker, Writing to Heal: A Guided Journal for Recovering from Trauma & Emotional Upheaval

Louise DeSalvo, Writing as a Way of Healing: How Telling Our Stories Transforms Our Lives

Stephen Lepore, The Writing Cure: How Expressive Writing Promotes Health and Emotional Well-Being.

Susan Zimmerman, Writing to Heal the Soul: Transforming Grief and Loss Through Writing

125

I want now to explore memoir and healing with respect to three of Mnemosyne's mythic associations. First, the idea of writing memoir as *imaginal* healing, as the gift of her father Ouranos. Secondly, the relationship of *physiological* healing to the crafting of memoir, as an intent of her mother Gaia. Thirdly, the idea of women's memoir as a *cultural* healing agent, one made possible by her daughters, the Muses. See Figure 3.

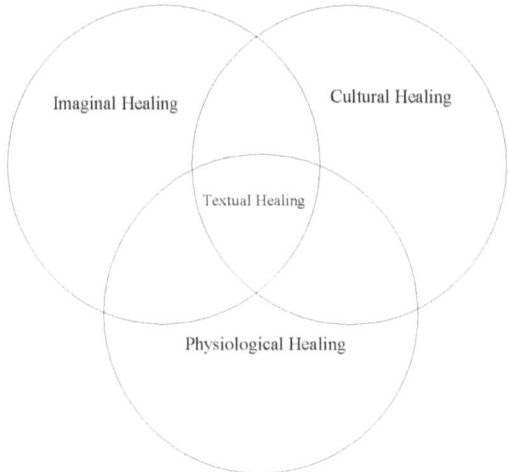

Figure 3

Imaginal Healing

James Hillman has followed both Henri Corbin and Carl Jung in developing an imaginal school of psychology that centers on the notion of the imaginal psyche. This approach emphasizes images as having their own existence and continuing to live on in the mind. In his book, *Healing Fiction,* Hillman describes psychoanalysis as "...a work of imaginative tellings in the realm of poesis, which simply means 'making' and which I take to mean *making by imagination into words.*" [181] He describes how psychotherapy set out to heal memory by identifying three steps in this process. First, the notion of memory as history is dismantled; second, remembrances are recognized as images; and third, a more poetic basis of mind is encouraged. He suggests that

...remembering goes on ... in modes of musing, in imagining, so that psychotherapy encourages musing, that activity which frees memories into images. As we muse over a memory, it becomes an image, shedding its literal historical facticity, slipping its causal chains, and opening to the stuff of which art is made. [182]

Hillman explains the way psychological case histories were initially written had much to do with the confluence of the new field of psychiatry and the prevailing literary genres of the day. He maintains Freud was tangled in both medical and literary genres while writing psychological case reports: "...fiction and case history; ever since then in the history of our field [psychology]...are inseparable; our case histories are a way of writing fiction." [183] As the founder of modern psychoanalysis, Freud's work became the template for how a case history was recorded. Because Freud associated himself with literature, Hillman maintains his "... histories are the stuff of fiction, they express the fictional side of human nature, its romance." [184] I am suggesting that a memoirist engages in a process similar to constructing a personal case history with the crafting of a memoir.

Hillman suggests that case histories are "fictions" in three senses: that such material is not a 'factual history' but rather a collection of psychological fantasies which are subjective recollections. As such, a case history describes psychic realities and does not place a rigid reliance on chronicity. He continues by pointing out the fictional nature of case history, observing how it is "...an invented account of imagined interior processes of a central character in a narrative story."[185] Finally, he notes a case history cannot be controverted or verified, and because of this, it is imagined as a set of mental constructs, fantasies by which one comes to understand the life experiences of a person. He goes on to suggest that psychology would do better to turn directly to literature as framework; as literature understands the psychology in fiction, psychology would do well to see the fiction in psychology. He points out the example of the picaresque mode in which a central figure does not develop, but goes through episodic, dis-continuous movements, experiencing tales within tales that go nowhere–just as psychic history goes on in many places at once.

> From the tragic perspective such a way [the picaresque]
> of framing a case history is a waste; soul demands
> something more metaphysically important. From the comic
> viewpoint there would have to be a resolution, some sort
> of accepting awareness and adaptation to the society which
> to the picaresque person is always hostile. From a heroic
> standpoint, the picaresque mode is a psychopathic parody of
> the individuation epic— but then individuation might be a
> paranoid organization of the picaresque. The same tale told
> as social realism would turn into a political tract.... [186]

He maintains that case histories have different fictional styles
and may be written in a variety of genres; therapy may be most
helpful when the person is aware of the multiplicity of viewpoints
which are available without having to choose one against the other.

Hillman observes that Freud was not as concerned with story as
with plot. For Freud, "...it is not the character and the story, or the
action that reveals what is going on: it is the plot of *psychodynamics.*
The characters are incidents of a universal plot and as such relatively
incidental."[187] In Hillman's assessment, "We are all, in this field
of psychotherapy, not medical empiricists, but *workers in story.*"[188]
We observe how a plot moves from asking the question of *"What
happened next?"* to *"Why did it happen?"* Hillman explains that
for the psychotherapists, theories about human behavior serve as
organizing plots. "They are the ways in which we put the intention
of human nature together so that we can understand the *why* between
the sequence of events in a story." [189] As the memoirist recollects
and constructs her narrative, she may begin with events initially
situated in time. Like Freud, she may be drawn to tell a particular
story with a particular chronology. However, as she reflects, time
falls away. Particular episodes call for deeper reflection, and her
writing becomes a means of making meaning of the events that she
has chosen to recount. She engages her imagination, and while the
story is an important organizing framework, it is the move to making
meaning that becomes the healing agent.

Hillman believes Freud's main aim with case histories was to
answer the *"why?"* but that his answer was fairly uniform for every
individual. The problem with Freud's identification of the Oedipus

myth, Hillman believes, is that it became a "mono plot," and human lives do not unfold side by side with this story only. Furthermore, the progression of one's life narrative and its plot are distinctly separate patterns. Freud's way of answering the "why" of human behavior depends solely on time sequences— what happened first, and what followed. Jung proposed there are other answers to "why" beyond causality. Hillman points out that Jung felt the question *"what for?"* was also implied, along with recognition of archetypal forces, myths, or persons —when attempting to understand a life narrative. Hillman explains that Jung's emphasis on the intentionality of the characters was critical to understanding. For Jung, the plot, (described by the theory of archetypes), is intrinsically variegated and multi-skeined. Individuation proceeds in many forms, has no prescribed momentum, and may come to no end.

Hillman reminds us that plots are myths; hence, the basic answers to the why of a human life can be discovered in myths. He describes how *mythos* is more than theory or plot, because it also calls up the interaction of the human and the divine. If one is in a myth, one is already linked to the divine powers. "The poetic basis of mind suggests that the selective logic operating in the plots of our lives is the logic of mythos, mythology." [190] As a person enters therapy, the diagnostic story provides a place to begin. Once it has been imagined as a particular clinical fantasy, one can begin to recall one's life with respect to the shape of that story, the past can then be re-told, perhaps one will even find a new internal coherence, even a sense of inevitability. "A diagnosis is indeed a *gnosis:* a mode of self knowledge that creates a cosmos in its image." [191] Hillman observes that the story one creates for one's self sets the tone for coping with life experiences; it is when the thematic motif breaks down that there is no longer a meaningful shape to the experiences of that life. The person is in search of a new story or a way of re-connecting with the old one. He asserts: "The way we imagine our lives is the way we are going to go on living our lives. For the manner in which we tell ourselves about what is going on is the genre through which the events become experiences." [192] Such musing is important for the memoirist since it validates the many threads in the tapestry of a life. For the memoirist, the plot of her life can be amplified and worked more deeply with the discovery of mythic themes and personages. Ultimately, there may be no single myth that organizes the person's narrative, but rather bits and pieces of many.

Hillman asserts that as we remember, we may create a narrative that might not have literally occurred but instead reflects how these events were internally experienced. This way of remembering things that "... never happened must rightly be called *imagining*, and this sort of memory is imagination. *Memoria* was the old term for both...the only difference between remembering and imagining was that memory images were those to which a sense of time had been added...."[193] Once memoria have been cut free from the need to be historical, they become archetypal, eternally present, not forgotten, not past, but present in the moment:

Our stories live in the details we recount, and the details tell the stories. The memoirist recounting trauma finds release in the expression of details, both literal and poetic. This need to construct a narrative can be paradoxical. While one's stories offer a sense of self, one can also fear these stories because through them one's imaginal foundation is exposed. Revelation of sexual trauma leaves one naked. It forces one to live through yet another stripping. It takes courage to write such events into memoir; it opens private musing for public inspection, setting the author to wonder how both the story and the meanings made from it will be received by the reader. Such writing may take years to surface. Maureen Murdock reminds us that "It is not easy to describe the details of pain or trauma at the time it is occurring; the process of healing has not yet begun. A writer needs time and distance to reflect upon her feelings." [194] The act of crafting a trauma narrative also becomes a means of affirming one's strengths, for as DeSalvo observes "...every survivor has them." [195] Memoir writing allows the writer time to muse over these difficult and formative events, and in the process, discover aspects of character which sustained her through the trauma and its aftermath.

While it may be that the raw story is the first to arrive on the page, once it is set down, the process of imagination is initiated. Images of the events which have demanded narration can be clarified and crafted as time passes. No longer in the present, the traumatic events can be contextualized and experienced as less threatening. Hillman speculates that perhaps these moves into history, into past tense, are a way of detaching, a means of separating an act from actuality, becoming something for reflection rather than for control. Events are "...now less affective and personal, more collective and general, part of a story rather than a report." [196]

Hillman observes the soul has a need to historicize, to place life events into a narrative form. He describes historicizing as a process that places events into another genre, neither in the present or once long ago, but a place in between, a place in the imagination.[197] He explains, "History enhances, dignifies. ... We historicize to give the events of our lives a dignity that they cannot receive from contemporaneousness. ...History dignifies because it moves events onto the stage of history, becoming thereby tragic, epic, and imaginative." [198] This move into the imaginal realm brings dignity to the personal recollections. Imagination allows one to observe at a distance, to see events as images:

> History is a way of musing upon oneself.....the possibility for revisioning and enhancing who we are lies within the events of each case history, if we learn to read it as fiction and its events as images of Memoria, and she needs remembering in order to create. [199]

Charlotte Perkins Gilmore, author of the 1892 short story "The Yellow Wallpaper" suffered from severe depression and was prescribed bed rest by both her doctor husband and subsequent doctors. Because her condition worsened, she went against their advice, resumed her writing and eventually left her marriage and changed her life. It was Gilmore's conviction that hysteria and depression are caused by not telling one's story. The self becomes furious at having its deepest needs rebuffed and subsequently begins to attack itself, to psychically self mutilate. She explained that her production of "The Yellow Wallpaper" was intended to help save others from being driven insane. Biographer Ann J. Lane states, "Perhaps one of the people she saved was herself, for in this story she seems to have let herself go, allowed her unconscious to help her creative art, and in so doing may have helped to purge the demons that terrified her... [and] achieved some control over both her illness and her past." [200]

It is through the use of metaphoric language, vehicles of the imagination, that recitation of traumatic events is possible.

> Because metaphors say one thing while meaning another, they are important vehicles for conveying information that seems beyond the limits of language. The metaphor compacts meaning, but it also evokes emotion, so it enables us to express nonliteral experiences in a highly individualized way. ...Creating metaphors and examining them...is healing because, by using these comparisons, we are forced to link events and feelings. [201]

One difficulty is finding language that can replicate the fragmentary, surreal, dissociated nature of the trauma. Surviving trauma often results in specific kinds of self-defense tactics. These may include blunting the emotions, experiencing a split of consciousness-as if the event were happening to someone else, or splitting the self into other personae. The challenge lies in finding forms which can convey these self-defensive tactics. Trying to tidy up the trauma into an organized, well-structured text may represent an unethical mode/stance in relation to the trauma inflicted. The forms in which these memories emerge are as much metaphor as the content itself. The imagination, once invited into the crafting of a memoir, will find unique ways to convey the events being named.

Hillman reminds us that the chief importance of the case history (or memoir), is that it provides

> ...a narrative, a literary fiction that de-literalizes our life from its projective obsession with outwardness by putting it into a story. They move us from the fiction of reality to the reality of fiction. They present us with the chance to recognize ourselves in the mess of the world as having been engaged and always being engaged in soul making ... [202]

The writing of a memoir may therefore also heal a person from her history by *freeing her imagination*. The memoirist need not continue in her own story as a victim of trauma, but as a person who has invited questions as to *why* and *what for*, a person who has wrested some meaning from the events experienced. Author Amy Tan articulates her experience of healing with writing thus:

> ...And so I rewrote, remembering what scared me: the ghosts, the threats, the curse. I wrote of wrong birth dates, secret marriages, the changing place one has in a family, the names that were nearly forgotten. I wrote of pain that reaches from the past, how it can grab you, how it can also heal itself like a broken bone. And with the help of my ghost writers, I found in memory and imagination what I had lost in grief. [203]

Memory heals into imagination if we persist. The writing of memoir invites a person to craft a soul story, to bear witness to the myth they are living, to name the gods/goddesses whom they have served.

Physiological Healing

Within the past twenty-five years there has been an increasing amount of research exploring the relationship between expressive writing and physiological healing from traumatic experiences. While all forms of psychotherapy have been shown to reduce stress and promote physical and mental well being, it has been suggested that the mere act of disclosure is a powerful therapeutic agent that may account for a substantial percentage of the variance in the healing process.[204]

James Pennebaker, a social psychologist, has been interested in the topic since the late 1970's. He began by studying the link between writing and wellness among college students, paying particular attention to writing about trauma and corresponding physiological changes. He designed a basic writing paradigm which asked participants to write on assigned topics for 3-5 consecutive days for periods of fifteen to thirty minutes a day. They were told to choose topics for writing which were to be considered "the most upsetting or traumatic experience of your life." [205] Individuals were encouraged to include as much detail as possible, including how this event had affected them in the past and present, as well as how they imagined it might affect them in the future.

Findings indicate that writing about trauma has very powerful consequences. Pennebaker's primary discoveries indicate that previously inhibited material can be dealt with successfully through expressive writing, resulting in improved physical health. He points out that inhibition, like other stressors, affects the immune system, the cardio-vascular system, as well as the biochemistry in the brain and nervous system. He outlines his framework for exploring inhibition and expression by noting that: 1) inhibition is physical work for the body, 2) inhibition affects short term biological changes and long term health, emphasizing the harder the body works at inhibiting, the greater the stress on the body, 3) inhibition impacts cognition; by not expressing an inhibited experience it remains un-assimilated, 4) Confrontation reduces the effects of inhibition, 5) Confrontation forces a re-thinking of events which in turn promotes integration of the experiences.[206]

Pennebaker maintains that when one begins to deal with un-assimilated events by putting them into words, describing our feelings and integrating them into our sense of self, there is no longer a need to work actively on inhibiting. The stress of holding back is dissipated and general health improves. His initial study further specified that in order to improve health, it wasn't enough to just write the events down; the writing must include detailed accounts which link feelings with events. The act of linking feelings with troubling events yields physical responses which parallel the effects of yoga/meditation; it is a process which helps create a more relaxed physiological state, evidenced by lower heart rates and improved antibody responses. In a 1996 study, Krantz and Pennebaker evaluated the difference between expression of traumatic experience using only expressive bodily movement, and writing and expressive bodily movement combined. Results indicated that it was only the combined expression group which demonstrated sustained health improvements in the months following the study. The authors of this study concluded that health gains appear to be closely related to the translation of the traumatic events into language. [207]

In a 1997 article for *Psychological Science*, Pennebaker summarized the results of sixteen separate studies on the effects of disclosure via expressive writing which manifested as overall reduction of physician visits, improved physiological markers including immune system serum levels, antibody levels, t-lymphocyte levels, liver enzyme levels, heart rate; improved behavioral markers including grade point average for students, re-employment following job loss, decrease in absenteeism from work, improved self reports in the areas of physical well being and reduction of stress, negative affect and depression. He concluded that when individuals are asked to write or talk about personal trauma in clinical experiments, consistent and significant health improvements occur. Effects are noted in both subjective and objective measurements of health and wellness. Further, the benefits seem to generalize across settings, the majority of individual differences and several Western cultural groups, and remain independent of social feedback.

Pennebaker postulates two possible reasons for the effectiveness of writing. The first possibility is related to the psychosomatic phenomenon of inhibition. Pennebaker has long been interested in the psychological effort required in the process of inhibiting painful life experiences. Such psychological effort is reflected in the physiological responses of the autonomic and central nervous system. Sustained over time, such behavior increases the risk of illness and other stress related disturbances. People who conceal traumatic past experiences [208] or who are judged as shy or withholding by their peers [209] tend to manifest more episodes of illness than those who are judged as not as inhibited. While inhibition appears to be a factor in long term health problems, the evidence that disclosure reduces these negative effects has not yet been conclusively demonstrated. [210] One study in 1992 noted that participants benefited equally from writing about traumas which had been previously disclosed in conversation as about those which they had kept secret. [211] The relationship between disclosure and improved long term physical health is intriguing, and studies continue in this area.

The second possibility as to why writing seems to create improved health is connected to the cognitive changes associated with it. The mere expression of trauma is not sufficient for changes in health; such gains appear to be related to translating such experiences into language. Pennebaker and his colleagues developed a computer-based language sampling/linguistic analysis technique aimed at evaluating the frequency and occurrence of a variety of emotional and psychological words used in writing studies.[212] Subsequent studies using this tool revealed three linguistic factors which seem to reliably predict improved physical health. The more the number of positive emotion words ("happy," "laugh"), the better subsequent health. A moderate number of negative emotion words ("sad," "angry") also predicted health. Third, an increase in causal and insight words ("understand," "realize") was strongly associated with improved health.[213] The organization of the narrative was also predictive of improved health, as those who benefited from the writing most began with poorly organized descriptions and progressed to more coherent stories by the time of the last writing exercise. Pennebaker notes that language analyses appear to offer promising tools for predicting long term health improvements from expressive writing activity. However, questions remain as to the degree to which cohesive stories/narratives predict changes in real-world cognitive processes: e.g., does a coherent story about trauma (as judged by what criteria?) produce improvements in health by reducing flashbacks and other PTSD symptoms? and does the creation of a narrative result in the assimilation of the previously unnamed experience, thereby allowing the individual to get on with living productively?

When one writes about specific trauma, one engages in a form of self care which promotes physical health. Consider the word *care* as the act of grieving, sorrowing, crying with. The etymology of *care* goes back to the Old Saxon word, *kara,* meaning grief and from Old High German *chara* meaning wail or lamentation. [214] Here the emphasis is on the importance of self-care because without such tending, we can place ourselves at risk of physical illness. Memoir can be viewed as a self-care tool which can improve both psychological and physiological health. Once the memoirist has found the words to express her experiences, the act of writing changes her "... relationship to [past events] and what they mean in the present. This is not done by language alone but by 'opening' the experience... that involves the entire bodily self." [215] As Mnemosyne's mythic image reminds us, memory lives in matter, specifically the matter of one's own body. Crafting a memoir can move experiences of trauma embedded in the body into another form, that of language.

Babette Rothschild, a psychotherapist specializing in trauma treatment, emphasizes the profound effect of body memory and its relationship to language:

> The body remembers traumatic events through the encoding in the brain of sensations, movements, and emotions that are associated with the trauma. Healing necessitates attention to what is happening in the body as well as the interpretations being made in the mind. Language bridges the mind/body gap, linking explicit and implicit memories. Somatic memory becomes personal history when the impact of the traumatic events are so weakened that the events can finally be placed in their proper point in the [person's] past. [216]

The act of writing serves as a bridge which opens the possibility of movement. Previously contained experiences of trauma are given both a new form and a new vehicle. It is not just the mind that is healed in the writing process, but the body as well. Once a narrative has been crafted, the writer experiences the strength required to recount the details, to tell the difficult parts of the stories. Not only has she felt in her body the weight of these stories and the pain of their details, but the physical sensations which follow their release. As Pennebaker has suggested, both carrying and releasing previously undisclosed stories involves physiological consequences. Our bodies record and react to both. DeSalvo reminds us that

> By writing, we celebrate, too, our courage and survival. Engaging in writing, in creative work, then, permits us to pass from numbness to feeling, from denial to acceptance, from conflict and chaos to order and resolution, from rage and loss to profound growth, from grief to joy. [217]

Cultural Healing

The idea of cultural healing through story telling is not new. In the western African tradition the *griot* serves as both keeper and giver of story, one who dispenses cultural medicine to society. By cultural medicine, I mean providing stories which inform the culture of its heritage, stories which bear witness to the events which shape it, keep it infused with shared images, and in so doing, keep it vital and healthy. I think that memoir functions in this manner, as the stories we receive and the stories we tell provide connection and healing not only for ourselves, but also the collective culture. The memoirist's work parallels that of the *griot/griotte*, as both work with stories offering cultural medicine. Writing is a particularly effective medium for the memoirist who wishes to bring her experiences into the culture's consciousness. Not only can memoir create apertures to experiences of trauma, but also to the myriad ways each of us experience daily events in our particular culture. Through memoir, as with the *griot/griotte's* stories, one can become reacquainted with one's heritage, just as the *griot/griotte's* provides the culture access to their ancestors and myths. Through selection of material, the time and place of its presentation, as well as to whom it is given, the culture is infused with stories which sustain it.

The term "time-binder" has been used to describe the *griot/griotte*, as such a person links the past to the present, as well as being a witness to current events, which he/she may or may not pass on to future generations. The stories of the *griot/griotte* provide access to understanding the values of the culture as well as its social structure. The *griot/griotte* renders history in multi-layered manner; they do not simply re-tell events. They make a "reading of the past for the audiences in the present, an interpretation that reflects a complex blend of both past and present values." [218] A memoirist performs the same kind of work as she renders her life narrative with the facets she chooses to include and the forms she selects for its presentation. She also makes an interpretation of her past, selecting the stories she deems necessary to pass on. She may choose to confront trauma directly, to name it and bring it out of the shadows, as Alice Sebold has done with *Lucky*. She may choose to "tell it slant" or omit the topic of trauma altogether. The interpretation she renders, both consciously and unconsciously, reflects her personal experiences as well as the culture in which she has developed, as Carolyn Steedman's *Landscape for a Good Woman* illustrates with her analysis of working class women in Great Britain. Japanese writer Kenzaburo Oe speaks to the conscious sharing of painful life events:

> ...we come to know despair—that dark night of the soul through which we have to pass, [which allows us to discover] ...that by actually giving it expression we can be healed and know the joy of recovering; and as these linked experiences of pain and recovery are added to one another, layer upon layer, not only is the artist [memoirist]'s work enriched, but its benefits are shared with others.[219]

Memoir is a malleable entity, one that can shape shift, both containing and reflecting the many experiences of our lives. While the recitation of personal narratives offers healing to the individual whose voice has not been heard, it also has the capacity to extend that healing to the collective culture that has historically excluded many voices. When Aurora Levins Morales describes writing as a defense against racism, I suggest her words could be equally applied as a defense of a person's voice,

> So the first and most important thing to understand is that we write from necessity; that our writing is a form of cultural and spiritual self-defense. To live surrounded by a popular culture in which we do not appear is a form of spiritual erasure that leaves us vulnerable to all assaults a society can commit against those it does not recognize. Not to be recognized, not to find oneself in history, or in film, or on television, or in books or in popular songs, or what is studied at schools leads to the psychic disaster of ceasing to recognize oneself.[220]

The healing capacity of memoir-crafting works in concentric rings. First, it has the potential to heal the sense of self; second, it has the potential to heal the listener/reader as the "I" disappears and is replaced by "we"; [221] third, it continues to push the evolution of contemporary women's writing, healing the form itself from previously rigid definitions; and lastly, the culture is healed from mono-perspectives by the sheer increase and inclusion of diverse voices. Imagined in this manner, memoir offers a way of healing the culture from the inside out.

Sharing one's work is an essential component in the process of writing to heal; if one writes the story and locks it away, one only repeats the lethal pattern of silencing, perpetuating the role of victim. While victims bear witness to the repressive and harmful actions and potentials within a culture, they do not serve to heal what is wrong. Rosaria Champagne explains:

> the difference between a survivor of violence and a victim of violence is the political meaning made of the traumatic experience....Victims become complicit with abuse and honor injunctions posed by the perpetrator to dismiss the abuse's import or impact. Survivors, in contrast, move to a place where they reject the demand to remain politely silent.[222]

Memoirs, particularly those that recount trauma and violence, point out the differences between viewing oneself as a survivor instead of a victim. Louise DeSalvo asserts:

> Survivors remember. Survivors speak up. Survivors speak out. Survivors tell stories. Survivors write and exchange them, sharing their meaning with an "interpretive community." But Survivors do this on their own terms, with the help they need, and when they are ready. [223]

Sharing trauma narratives raises awareness as to the diversity and multiplicity of experiences within a culture at a given point in time. It challenges old notions of what kinds of behavior, specifically violence and infliction of trauma, are acceptable and expected. It gives pause, by reminding its audience of the possibilities of violence with which we all live, and how we might respond should it erupt in our own lives. DeSalvo observes:

> Storytelling teaches or re-teaches us empathy. This trait is a prerequisite for treating others well. But it depends upon our ability to imagine what it feels like to be another person.

We do this through storytelling. Because the capacity for empathy is often lost in extreme situations, restoring empathy in survivors is essential. Writing is one important way to accomplish this.[224]

While memoir can be a tool that changes the cultural imagination with regard to the meaning of "survivor" versus "victim," it can lead to yet another consideration: that of "witness." Being a survivor implies an individual's tensile strength and capacity for surviving, but it doesn't really concern itself with the concentric rings of others and the surrounding culture. Shifting perspective from victim to survivor to that of witness, "...means taking on the responsibility of telling what happened to us—writing a historical record, a public document....(the) witness offers testimony to a truth that is generally unrecognized or suppressed," according to Arthur W. Frank.[225] Morales echoes this sentiment, "Healing takes place in community, the telling and the bearing witness, in the naming of trauma and in the grief and rage and defiance that follow." [226] While the healing that comes from writing may start in solitude, it is completed in the presence of others; not only is the writer's experience mirrored back to her, but her audience is able to see the parts of her experiences in themselves. In this dance of broken mirrors, a new kind of wholeness is achieved.

Comparative literature scholar Shoshana Felman poses several questions with regard to textual witnessing and construction of personal narratives:

> How is the act of writing tied up with the act of *bearing witness*...? Is the act of reading literary texts itself inherently related to the act of facing horror? If literature is the alignment between witnesses, what would this alignment mean? And by virtue of what sort of agency is one appointed to bear witness? [227]

These questions expand and complicate the memoirist's task. She bears witness to her own experiences, as well as the culture's influence on both her life events and the sense she makes of them. Through the vehicle of her narrative, she offers a threshold to her reader, one which may invite the reader to face a trauma that could otherwise be avoided. In the act of recording trauma, the reader is called to accountability: "Now that you know this story, how will you live?" Ultimately, it is the memoirist who shoulders these decisions, who decides which stories are the ones to pass on. Felman states the solemnity of witness; "To bear witness is to bear the solitude of a responsibility, and to hear the responsibility, precisely of that solitude." [228] She goes on to emphasize how the witness addresses others, which results in the witness becoming an actual "... vehicle of an occurrence, a reality, a stance or a dimension beyond [ones] self." [229] Memoir can also be imagined as such a vehicle; the stories of the ancestors and the culture itself are behind each word, much like an artist's pentimento.

Psychoanalyst Dori Laub notes three levels of witnessing in relation to Holocaust [trauma] experience; the level of being a witness to oneself within the experience, (autobiographical experience), the level of being a witness to the testimony of others (listening to a first person account of the trauma), and the level of being a witness to the process of witnessing itself, a process between the listener and speaker which alternates between moving closer and moving away from the traumatic experience.[230] In this last level of witnessing, the listener understands the speaker's need to tell, as well as the need to retreat so as to reflect on these memories. This process helps to reassert the truth of the experiences and to build new links and assimilations to the present moment.

> The survivors did not only need to survive so that they could tell their stories, they also needed to tell their stories in order to survive. There is, in each survivor, an imperative need to tell and thus to come to know one's own story, unimpeded by ghosts from the past against which one has to protect oneself. One has to know one's buried truth in order to be able to live one's life. [231]

The memoirist is engaged in the same dance of healing and meaning making. The traumas of a life require a recounting. In crafting stories the memoirist begins to find the patterns of her life, to see herself in relationship to formative events, her family, and culture. It is a brave dance, because there are no guarantees as to the outcomes. Healing may not occur in the ways one may expect. Laub articulates the paradox and pain entwined with standing up and speaking one's experience of trauma as follows:

> ... the act of bearing witness at the same time both makes and breaks a promise: the promise of the testimony as a realization of the truth. On the one hand, the process of the testimony does in fact hold out the promise of truth as the return of a sane, normal, and connected world. On the other hand, because of its very commitment to truth, the testimony enforces at least a partial breach, failure and relinquishment of this promise. The mother that comes back not only fails to make the world safe for the little boy as she promised, but she comes back different, disfigured, not identical to herself. She no longer looks like the mother in the picture. There is no healing reunion with those who are, and continue to be, missing, no recapture or restoration of what has been lost, no resumption of an abruptly interrupted innocent childhood.
>
> ...It is the realization that the lost ones are not coming back; the realization that what life is all about is precisely living with unfulfilled hope; only this time with the sense that you are not alone any longer—that someone can be there as your companion—knowing you, living with you through the unfulfilled hope, someone saying: "I'll be with you in the very process of your losing me. I am your witness." [232]

The memoirist offers her culture healing, much like a modern day *griotte*. She selects the stories to pass on, shining light on her personal experiences of violence and trauma. As she presents her stories, the culture's consciousness is enriched by the inclusion of both more and diverse perspectives. She challenges her culture to wrestle with the dilemmas of those they place on the margins. She challenges her audience to understand more deeply the nuances of victim, survivor, and witness. She inspires them with her ability to survive, to make meaning of her experiences, and calls them to do the same. She both carries and transmits the challenge of rethinking how one participates in the larger culture as the result of her personal experiences. Each writer presents her witness with her own unique voice, each offering a fractal of what it means to be a human being in contemporary time, each carrying the community building and healing intents of the Muses.

Crafting our stories, particularly those of traumatic events, can heal us imaginally, physically, and culturally. Mnemosyne's work heals the intangible, airy stuff of memory into imagination. She heals the very matter of our bodies by finding a place in language for what was previously held in blood, bone, and muscle. She offers the potential of cultural healing by giving witness to both personal traumas and the traumas others, calling her audience to consider their response and how to live in the world with compassion, intelligence, and dignity.

Chapter Six:
Meeting in the middle: An Imaginal Field

It is human nature to imagine, to put yourself in another's shoes. The past may be another country. But the only passport required is empathy.

— Geraldine Brooks, "Timeless Tact" in *Writers on Writing*

What is it that our story wants? It keeps coming to the tip of our tongue. It rushes into empty spaces and flees from unhearing ears. It repeats itself, filling out each detail, trying to become real to us. It wants the other to dwell with it, to question, to ask for repetitions, to be made still by it. We rush in with some insignificant fact to relieve the silence, as we secretly wish the other to bring us back—to say that the silence was not empty, that it was filled with our experience, that it was given a place, and that the span of time marked its reality. We want to "get it across" from this space, to that between, to the other. It seeks to move one, to be known, to establish itself. When the other ceases to offer hope or advice, when they listen to our tale for no ulterior motive of their own, when they are still and can yet be moved... then something happens. The experience we are recounting connects us. It lives with us. It is what at that one moment makes us live. It thereby becomes real in a new sense.

—Mary Watkins, *Waking Dreams*

In my writing room, I go back into the past, to that moment when my grandmother told my mother not to follow her footsteps. My grandmother and I are walking side by side, imagining the past differently, remembering it another way. Together we come upon a tomb of memories. We open it and release what has been buried for too long—the terrible despair, the destructive rage. We hurt, we grieve, we cry. And we see what remains: the hopes, broken to bits but still there.

I look at the photograph of my grandmother. Together we write the stories of things that were and shouldn't have been, or could have been, or might still be. We know the past can be changed. We can choose what to believe. We can choose what to remember. That is what frees us, this choice, frees us to hope that we can redeem these same memories for the little girl who became my mother.

— Amy Tan, *The Opposite of Fate*

Now let's consider the last aspect of the Venn diagram, the center. It is here where content, form, and use intersect and create a central aperture, a place where writer and reader meet, a place for the reader to step over the threshold of the Other's, the memoirist's reality. This aperture becomes a window which provides an inside-out kind of view from within a particular life, offering a viewpoint which has been steeped in its own unique soup of experiences and cultural norms. The center can be further imagined as a dynamic intersection where something new emerges, a place where the reader meets the writer and a new field of understanding is created. In this place, both the writer and reader are opened to new possibilities, to shifts in perspectives, as well as the many interrelationships which weave a particular memoir. When considering one's life narratives, this intersection is the realm of an *imaginal field*. On first glance, one understands this is where the reader meets the particular memoirist as an 'Other.' Upon further reflection, it is also reveals itself as the place where the memoirist simultaneously entertains the others in the self, including the ancestors. As she explores her personal lineage, she invites their presence, and gives voice to their stories and experiences.

I think of this discussion as a set of nested circles. The outermost ring is where memoir creates an opportunity to stand on the threshold of an Other, in order to increase awareness and empathy within and beyond one's own realm of personal experience. The next nested circle includes the place where we meet the Others in the self, followed by the Ancestors. The innermost circle is where Mnemosyne lives, offering her story and associations as inspiration for the memoirist. See Figure 4.

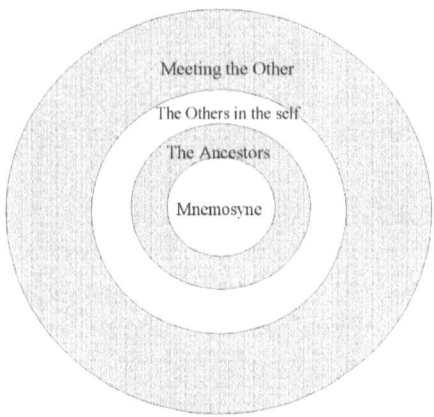

Meeting the Other

The Others in the self

The Ancestors

Mnemosyne

Figure 4

Meeting the Other

Memoir offers a way into another life as well as other cultures. It is a way to meet an Other, someone we perceive as different from ourselves. As the planet moves toward a greater shared global economy, sharing literature cross-culturally becomes more common if not imperative. The impulse both to write and read memoir seems to resonate across national and geographic boundaries. Human beings are story tellers and thus require an audience. Comparative mythologist Wendy Doniger observes

Behind a narrative is an experience, real or imagined: something has happened—not once like a historical event, but many times, like a personal habit. Narrative does not receive raw experience and then impose a form upon it. Human experience is inherently narrative; this is our primary way of organizing and giving coherence to our lives.[233]

It is this impulse to both create and receive narrative, narrative derived from personal experience, which offers hope for human understanding, one story at a time. Jill Kerr Conway suggests:

...We want to know how the world looks from inside another person's experience, and when that craving is met by a convincing narrative, we find it deeply satisfying. The satisfaction comes from being allowed *inside* the experience of another person who really lived and who tells about experiences which did in fact occur. In this way the lost suspension of disbelief disappears and the reader is able to try on the experience of another, just as one would try on a dress or suit of clothes, to see what the image in the mirror then looks like. When we read about a totally disparate experience, say as Christians reading about a life lived by a believer in Islam, it is as though the set designer and the lighting specialist provided us with a totally different scene and pattern of light and shadows to illuminate the stage on which we live our lives. [234]

Through the vehicle of the memoir, the reader is able to stand at another's threshold. She is also given the opportunity to cross over, to enter that realm of experience, to take in the sights and sounds and then weigh them against her own life experiences. When the reader has those moments of recognition of something familiar, the memoirist is no longer a stranger but someone else who has had similar sensations, conversations, heart aches, and joys. Amy Tan describes how the writing and reading of memoir serve to make connections and offer hope.

I also think of reading as an act of faith, a hope I will discover something remarkable about an ordinary life, about myself.

And if the writer and reader discover the same thing, if they have that connection, the act of faith has resulted in an act of magic. To me, that's the mystery and wonder of both life and fiction—the connection between two unique individuals who discover in the end that they are more the same than they are different. And if that doesn't happen, it's nobody's fault. There are still plenty of other books on the shelf to choose from. [235]

Because memoir offers an opportunity for understanding an individual life as it emerges from a particular culture, it has much in common with the field of anthropology. The anthropologist, according to Karen McCarthy Brown, seeks to understand a particular culture's "way of making meaning in the world." [236] The memoirist also conveys the local and particular aspects of her culture as she constructs her narrative. She attempts to make sense of her own experience, and to consider the layers of relationship and public events against which her story unfolds. In *Mama Lola*, McCarthy Brown acknowledges the multi-layers of analysis involved in an endeavor of ethnography, a kind of narrative that can parallel a memoir.

> ...an ethnography is written by making meaning of others' processes of meaning making.... I was engaged in learning about Second Diaspora people, Haitians whose ancestors were forcibly removed from Africa by slave traders, and who more recently were forced to leave Haiti by poverty and political upheaval. As if that were not enough, these culturally complex people were also actively engaged in trying to make sense of my own culture at the same time and in the same places that I was trying to make sense of theirs.[237]

Such a description could also be attributed to a memoirist who seeks to articulate her personal search for meaning, her history, the culture of her ancestors, and the politics of the day. She writes in a kind of tri-partite awareness: the experience in the past, the present moment, and the possibilities of the future. McCarthy Brown wrote a complex and many faceted view of the culture of Vodou by exploring the life of a particular Vodou priestess in Brooklyn, New York. Her ethnography has been described as "postmodern" due to the many voices in the text, the presence of the author's personal experiences, and the written presentation of 'imaginal' family stories. While her focus is scholarly investigation, it is also an intriguing demonstration of the blurred lines of contemporary women's narratives. McCarthy Brown contends that such a work could only be presented via multiple perspectives. She saw her task as one of collecting "...the chorus of voices, [and] it became clear that my role was to be the conductor. It was my job to see that each voice got heard." [238] This methodology challenges more traditional anthropological research which tries to keep a more critical distance between the researcher and subjects, but it seems much at home with the evolution of life narratives.

With the inclusion of personal narrative, much in the style of memoir, McCarthy Brown also addresses the concerns of feminist scholar Rosalind Shaw in that she attempts to incorporate more reflexivity, more attention to intersubjectivity, more attention to the voices of other women, and more attention to the web of social relationships/practices which constitutes women's source of power.[239] McCarthy Brown's work seeks to make contemporary women's stories seen and heard. By including her own voice and experience, she demonstrates the importance of first person narrative. She creates a threshold and offers a textual immersion in the experience of Vodou in the United States. *Mama Lola* conveys the complexities of content, form, and uses of contemporary narratives.

Helen Epstein's *Where She Came From* provides another example of how multiple skeins of history, cultural studies, sociology, and politics can be woven into contemporary memoir. As the daughter of a Holocaust survivor, Epstein possessed very few family documents. Upon the death of her mother, she was compelled to research and document her maternal lineage. In order to learn the stories of these women and, in turn, better understand herself, she began to piece together a narrative of the lives of the women of her family set against a background of social history of Central European Jews. She traveled to Czechoslovakia, Israel, and Austria in search of family connections over a twelve year period. Bits and pieces of family stories served as compass points. Her great-grandmother was a Moravian inn keeper's daughter who fell in love with a Christian Czech, but was compelled to enter an arranged marriage with a Jewish peddler. She eventually committed suicide by throwing herself from a window. Throughout the memoir Epstein weaves the specific history of her ancestors against the backdrop of both Central European and Jewish history. She offers the reader a view of Central European Jewish culture beginning with the emergence of the community from the ghettos as laws were more liberalized; she then follows the trend of assimilation into Central European Culture, and explores the experiences of those of Jewish culture during the first Czech Republic. She describes in detail what occurred to the Jews, including those who considered themselves "converted," with the 1939 occupation by Nazi forces. Epstein is primarily concerned with women's history and how the changes in social and political climates affect the lives of her great-grandmother, grandmother and mother. She examines the meaning of Jewish-ness within her own family and finds the full range of practice, from those who were devoutly religious Jews to those who assimilated without fanfare into the existing culture. She also spends time exploring the effects of the early woman's movement on the women in her family, observing how her foremothers were self-supporting in a time and place when this was not common.

Her work offers a description of Central European Jewish life that has not been previously available, since most records have been presented from a Western European point of view. She further explores attitudes toward Jews in the Czech Republic and Austria over several generations and then weaves in the narrative of the fortunes of her own family. Through her grandmother's eyes, she captures the feelings of so many Jews of her day, and how they were simply unable to grasp the horror of the Hitler's threat. Epstein simultaneously grapples with the personal loss of her mother and with the larger past, reverberating with all the devastation of the Holocaust.

At the conclusion of her memoir, she visits the grave of her great-grandmother in a Jewish Cemetery, symbolically planting a pot of flowers she hopes will take root. Epstein demonstrates that European Jewish history is not yet obliterated, that narratives can be constructed, even with the tiniest of remnants. Furthermore, such narratives can offer a renewed sense of rootedness, of cultural heritage previously thought to be lost. Such a memoir offers a threshold to the Others of preceding generations, to the Others who lived through the Holocaust, the Others who learned to reinvent themselves in a new country

The contemporary memoirist paints a story of her culture from the inside out, conveying an intimate, imaginal field of experience for the reader. While the reader may not share the same blood lines that carried these particular stories forward, the memoir can nonetheless serve as a threshold and a bridge, a place where appreciation of the Other can begin. A memoir provides a way of representing perspectives, of opening borders between people and cultures, making an opportunity for images to meet one another. It is in the imagination that shifts in perspective occur. The Other is now no longer wholly "other" after her story has been received. The reader of memoir can no longer deny the writer's shared humanity, her personal challenges and victories. A filament of connection has been established, even a sense of responsibility for having witnessed in text another's life. Such filaments, like the fiber optic network of the world wide web, are portals for future conversation and exchange. Mary Watkins, an imaginal psychologist, emphasizes how "the interpenetration of imaginal dialogues with oneself, one's neighbors, within one's community, between communities, and with the earth and its creatures" [240] is a way of visioning the healing of self, culture and world. She explains how genuine "dialogue is the method for this hosting, penetration, and holding of difference." [241] Memoir is one such way to begin a dialogue, as well as a way to sustain and deepen the conversation.

Contemporary Narratives and the Imagination

More and more contemporary memoirs feel free weave fantasies of the writer into the narrative. This exploration of fantasy of the inner world of the writer emphasizes the creative power of the imagination to construct the story. In this style of writing, the imaginal field is entered through the "reality" of the writer's imagination and fantasies, a place where the imagination is experienced as offering its own kind of truth. Maxine Hong Kingston's *The Woman Warrior* stands as an example of the importance of the imagination in a contemporary woman's process of constructing a narrative. She considers many possible perspectives in constructing a narrative of her maternal ancestors, realizing that such perspectives refract within her own life, shaping her personal range of viewpoints.

Given the number of women's memoirs published within the past twenty years that include fiction-like segments, it would seem there has been an increased recognition and acceptance of the imagination in the construction of memoir. Such recent works as Isabella Allende's *Paula,* and Terry Tempest William's *Leap* present fiction-like vignettes, shaped by a set of aesthetics which value atmosphere, feelings, and psychological insights. The continued presentation of imaginal sequences in memoir affirm the significance of the writer's inner freedom and demonstrate the engagement of imagination with the kinds of reflections and the various inflections of the Muses. It would seem that integrating the imagination into memoir writing yields a greater flexibility and creativity, which results in a kind of melding of subject matter, personality, and form.

Isabel Allende's memoir, *Paula*, an account of the year in which her daughter was stricken by a rare disease and left in a coma, is a vivid example of how one woman's imagination creates an inner realm for coping with tragedy. Allende alternates between addressing her daughter, describing her family members, recalling the political turmoil in Pinochet's Chile and her years in exile, and ruminating on the events that brought her to writing, and arguing with the mystery of life. Gradually, the myth of Demeter and Persephone emerges as her template for learning to release the daughter she so deeply loves. Allende comes to understand it was her lot as a mother, like Demeter, to travel the depths of her private underworld before she could make sense of her daughter's death. As the memoir draws to a close, she includes dream images of Paula, who, like Persephone, begs her mother to let her go. In the memoir's final scene, Allende recounts another dream in which she climbs a tower with her daughter, flying out over the countryside with her, eventually landing in a stream and dissolving into the fresh water. Through the recitation of the dreamscape, Allende makes peace with the finality of her daughter's death and has an epiphany about their continued connectedness in the web of all being. Her prose provides a powerful example of the intersection of women's imagination and memory, and of how difficult life experiences can be conveyed in the language of reverie.

Amy Tan, much in the spirit of Allende, describes her experience of memory, imagination and writing thus,

> When I write my stories, I do not use childhood memories. I use a child's memory. Through that child's mind, I am too inexperienced to have assumptions. So the world is still full of magic. Anything can happen. All possibilities. I have dreams. I have fantasies. At will, I can enter that world again.[242]

Tan describes how her memory and imagination become a process of synthesis, and how for her, "...writing from memory is more about remembering my psychological place in the world at different stages." [243] She describes her awareness of the subjectivity of her memories, and how this kind of malleability is both "...the most unreliable and most authentic element a writer can infuse into her work." [244] These kind of reflections continue the theme of conscious engagement with the imagination in contemporary memoir.

An Imaginal Field

I like to think of this dynamic intersection created by content, form, and use as an 'imaginal' field because it best captures the idea of a place different from that of the dichotomy of real-unreal. Henri Corbin introduced the idea of the 'imaginal' as a realm of image that exists on an equal footing with the realm of bodily sensation and the realm abstract intellect based on his studies of Arabic and Persian texts.[245] He describes it as an "intermediary world," a world of "subtle bodies," a place between our ordinary ideas of physical sensation and intellectual ideas. The imaginal realm is a place where consciousness moves, one that invites consideration and shifts in perspective.

James Hillman, in *Re-Visioning Psychology,* recalls C.G. Jung's work and explains how images are the psyche's mode of presentation and how such images inform one's life:

> Jung's position here states that the fundamental facts of existence are the fantasy images of the psyche. Everything else—ideas of the mind, sensations of the body, perceptions of the world around us, beliefs, feelings, hungers,—must present themselves as images in order to be experienced. "'Experience' is in its most simple form, an exceedingly complicated structure of mental images." Should we ask: just what *is* psyche? What do you mean by psychic experience and reality? The answer is fantasy images. "Image *is* psyche," says Jung. "Psyche consists essentially of images... a picturing of vital activities."

> In the beginning is the image; first imagination then perception; first fantasy then reality. Or as Jung puts it "The psyche creates reality everyday. The only expression I can use for this activity is fantasy." Man is primarily an image maker and our psychic substance consists of images; our being is imaginal being, an existence in imagination. We are indeed such stuff as dreams are made on.[246]

Hillman calls for a way of being in the world that goes beyond earlier definitions of psychology. For him, psychology is a means of cultivating the soul. He maintains such cultivation "... calls for dreaming, fantasying, imagining. To live psychologically means to imagine things; to be in touch with soul means to live in sensuous connection with fantasy. To be in soul is to experience the fantasy in all realities and the basic reality of fantasy." [247] The memoirist who approaches her writing in this manner will give voice to the images that present themselves as she seeks to construct her narrative. She will not be compelled to present a linear recitation of facts, but instead, entertain the associations and flights her stories take. Indeed, the memoirist values this imaginal world, one that Robert Romanyshyn describes as apparent "... only to a vision that sees through the facts and penetrates the veil of ideas with which the mind clothes the world." [248] The memoirist takes to heart the value of reverie, the images it engages, the feelings it evokes. Such a way of writing deepens the stories she crafts, adding resonance and depth to her narrative. Romanyshyn continues:

> Suspending for a moment the facts which we have about things and the ideas which we know of them, mysteries are born. Reverie, Bachelard notes, enlarges our lives "by letting us in on the secrets of the universe." In moments of reverie, I wonder about facts and reasons. What are they? Facts are about things, and things that have what a colleague and friend of mine once called "punchability." I can count facts and can count on them. They yield themselves to measurement and observation. Water is H_2O. That is a fact. Sunlight is a spectrum of colors. That is a fact. ... But between matter and mind, between matters of fact and ideas of reason, there is a whole other universe where the poet dwells, a domain of reality that yields its secrets to an aesthetic sensibility.[249]

Virginia Woolf observes how the real often draws attention to itself in the matter at hand; the matter of human construction, the matter of social events, the matter of nature itself. Imagination is the spark that illuminates each moment of the real; such moments for the writer are mutually informed by both matter and mind.

> What is meant by reality? It would seem to be something very erratic, very undependable—now to be found in a dusty road, now in a scrap of newspaper in the street, now a daffodil in the sun. It lights up a group in a room and stamps some casual saying. It overwhelms one walking home beneath the stars and makes the silent world more real than the world of speech—and then there it is again in an omnibus in the uproar of Piccadilly. Sometimes, too, it seems to swell in shapes too far away for us to discern what their nature is. [250]

Mary Watkins describes how an imaginal kind of psychology opens one to the myriad possibilities in each moment. Her interests focus on

... a psychology itself derived from our experience with imaginal movements. As we learn to recognize images and to allow them to teach us their ways of imagining, we will discover that each of our actions, feelings, perceptions, and thoughts can be used to approach the imaginal... and that, indeed, our attention to the imaginal movements of daily life can enrich and deepen our connection to that life. [251]

James Hillman expands the imaginal mode further by proposing the idea of *personification*. He describes this psychological activity as "a mode of thought" ...an act we perform while being present to our experiences. [252] "Personifying is a way of being in the world as *experiencing the world as a psychological field*, where persons are given with events so that the events are experiences that touch us, move us, appeal to us." [253] Such an imaginal approach works well for the memoirist who is interested in recollected persons, images and fragments of experience. Often the story one sets out to tell isn't the same story that wants to be told. Flannery O'Connor notes this need to be open to the possibilities when she underscores the importance of entering the story-cape as more of a naturalist-observer.

As soon as the writer learns to write, as soon as he knows what he is going to find, and discovers a way to say he knew it all along, or worse still, a way to say nothing, he is finished. If a writer is any good what he makes will have its source in a realm much larger than that which his conscious mind can encompass and will always be a greater surprise to him than it can ever be to his reader.[254]

The memoirist sets out to capture an event that was meaningful, that for some reason won't let go until it has been set to text. If she listens closely, other images cluster around the one she has set her sights on, each image adding complexity and texture to the story she is attempting to create. Watkins describes how an image can function like a magnet, layering further images and associations as one reflects upon it.

Think of a poem or a piece of music that you read or hear over and over again. ... Layer upon layer, one image comes into being with you. It comes not just on its own—as a single set of words on paper—but rather as the poem streams through you, it collects likeness among the other images of your soul. It draws to it cast out memoria, landscapes (actual and imaginal), emotions. It ferrets out your hopes and fears. All this it pulls through you separating out some as the image becomes more specific, drawing more along as it widens. The poem pulls you into its world through your own world. [255]

Adrienne Rich tells of an encounter with a Great Blue Heron as she returned home from an errand. She had never seen one in such close proximity, and felt compelled to speak out loud to it. The moment was riveting. After the bird flew off, Rich tells of her need to verify its name, to stay with the image she had just seen. In the process of researching the bird, her eyes traveled the margins of the reference book that lists all the other creatures common to the Pacific coastline of North America. She felt herself pulled by the many other names of creatures, which led her into a reverie of the whys and hows of naming things in the natural world:

...The eye for likeness in the midst of contrast, the appeal to recognition, the association of thing to thing, spiritual fact with embodied form, begins here. And so begins the suggestion of multiple, many layered, rather than singular, meanings, wherever we look, in the ordinary world. [256]

As she follows the image of the Great Blue Heron, it leads her to other associations; the fractured relationship between poetry, science and politics, the specific intelligence of the bird that could never be fully known by a human, the resistance to claiming a special message in the tradition of a Native American spirituality, from the encounter. She describes how her imagination seemed to come into focus with the encounter and then grow more associative with the image of the bird. In the end, she concludes by acknowledging

...our trajectories crossed at time when I was ready to begin to see something new, the nature of which I did not clearly see. And poetry, too, begins this way: the crossing of trajectories of two (or more) elements that might not otherwise have known simultaneity. When this happens, a piece of the universe is revealed as if for the first time. [257]

Rich knows that in writing about her encounter with the Heron, there will be more to the story than just *that* moment. In following her associations, and her un-willingness to engage the bird as an "other" or as a messenger, she chooses instead to engage the imaginal through the vehicle of words. "... I needed to acknowledge the heron with speech, and by confirming its name. To it I brought the kind of thing my kind of creature does." [258] Rich's reverie on the Blue Heron demonstrates approaching the imaginal through words themselves brings fresh insights, new ways to exress the wonder of a human experience.

Mary Watkins describes a variety of portals to imagining, suggesting each one can be understood as resulting from various processes of transforming awareness. She suggests each of the following as different ways of imagining;

1) you are watching images but are not yourself among the images. You as you know yourself, are the one watching

2) You see yourself watching the images from within the imaginal scene. For example, you see yourself looking down from a tree

3) You see yourself interacting with the images within the landscape of the imagination

4) You are within the scene watching the images (you yourself are in the tree)

5) You are interacting with images within the landscape of the imagination as yourself

6) You are interacting with other images in an imaginal body not your own. You are still willing your actions.

7) You are interacting within the imaginal landscape but not as you usually would. Your actions are not initiated from your conscious ego. *You* are moved, as well as the rest of the images.

8) You are interacting within the imaginal landscape not as yourself but as a peripheral image to the scene. For example, you are the tree and being the tree are in touch with the other images around the tree. You do not think what the tree is going to do. You are what ever the tree does.

9) You are an image. You are not in your imaginary ego or body. You feel and move and are the ground or a bird. You are not your normal ego in the bird's body. You are the bird.

10) You are watching the images from within the imaginal scene but the you that is watching them is a different kind of ego with different ways of perceiving and movement than we notice at first.
—from *Waking Dreams*,114.

Imaginal portals are useful for the memoirist who attempts to recall events from other perspectives. They provide a means of entering and expressing events that may resist a more linear or literal re-telling. Any one of these ways of entering the imaginal offers an opportunity to begin a story, to find the images and relationships which want to be named. Watkins goes on to emphasize the importance of deepening the context of an image, ".... By spending time with it, trying to feel it, to slip into it, we can try to note where and how it lives. How does it spend a day? What is its sense of time?"[259]

Such an approach to writing memoir requires patience and softer, more poetic, eyes. The story one is compelled to write assumes its own center, its own force of character. Once an image is met, a memoir can begin. The image, like pollen, is fertile. Once encountered, it germinates in the mind and heart of the writer who brings it into form. If the memoirist can tend what emerges, it will yield sustenance for both writer and reader. Adrienne Rich also notes how the imagination can lead to transformation, if the writer has the courage to consider new possibilities, other vantages points.

> ...if the imagination is to transcend and transform experience, it has to question, to challenge, to conceive of alternatives, perhaps the very life you are living at that moment. You have to be free to play around with the notion that day might be night, love might be hate, nothing can be too sacred for the imagination to turn to its opposite or call experimentally by another name. For writing is re-naming. [260]

Meeting the Others in the self

Memoir offers the writer a unique opportunity for meeting the Others in the self. What starts out as a simple desire to set an event to paper soon enough confronts one with the Others who are part of the story. With the passage of time, these Others become *the writer's* versions of the people who were present in the original events. They live in one as images and become bound up with one's memories of various life experiences. Such is how mythic consciousness operates. While the memoirist tries to present these Others as clearly as possible, she realizes the persons of memory and the persons yet living may be in fact, dissimilar. People change over time. As the memoirist is able to note the shifts in her own world view, her own set of character traits, she becomes aware that these Others may have also experienced such shifts in world view and personality. She may even begin to entertain the idea that the characters in her memory have their own views, their own interests in the story at hand. Watkins imaginal psychology would have one consider the characters as active participants in the construction of the story. "The characters we meet implore us to listen to them for a change, to follow or be taken by them to unfamiliar places, leaving our habitual conceptions as to who we are, what reality is." [261] She further describes how our images carry their own unique character and way of expressing themselves, serving as guides if we are patient with them.

> Each image discloses its own character—the particular way it shapes and expresses the nature of the imaginal—by being itself. It tells what it is doing by doing it, by acting itself out. ... It does not seem likely that we can say all images intend to teach us, but we can say that by dwelling with all images we can learn something of them. [262]

C.G. Jung named the process of engaging this kind of conscious relationship with such figures as "active imagination." This notion was meant to encourage the individual to take an active part in the encounter with one's various unconscious archetypal images. As a technique, Robert Hopcke explains, active imagination is meant to serve as a conduit "between passive, receptive awareness of inner unconscious material and active, elective responding to this material in whatever form"[263] Jung suggested one enter a state of reverie, preserving a sense of observing without judgment. He encourages one to pay attention to what fantasies or images emerged, to note the movements of the images while taking care not to interfere with the scenes as they unfolded. He further suggests one try to bring the fantasies into some kind of form, through paint, paper, and various art materials.[264]

For the memoirist, active imagination can be a helpful tool in discovering the characters of one's own story and what they would like to say. Watkins reminds us that as characters become more highly specified, more discrete in their identities, it is precisely their particularity that helps differentiate the multiplicity of perspectives so important for thought, literature, and myth. She notes further how "Both in acting and in fiction-writing [memoir construction], the actor or writer becomes absorbed in the details of the imaginal other's character, life, and point of view."[265] The use of active imagination provides the memoirist more openings to her story, more perspectives, more ways of recounting experience. The end result is not a narrator with a single perspective but a narrator "attuned to and respectful of the multiplicity of the self." [266] Hillman describes such an approach as a means of saving "the diversity and autonomy of the psyche from dominion by any single power." [267] Memoir written in this mode parallels the shift in modern literature where the omniscient narrator has become a less prevalent figure, where narrators often join an assembly of characters whose perspectives are also fallible. [268]

In the practice of active imagination, imaginal dialogues are another means of cultivating relationships with imaginal figures or characters. As one engages this practice, the characters become more released, more autonomous, more articulated, more differentiated through their multiplicity. Watkins maintains that "Interactions with these figures proceed from monologue to dialogue— to relations which are reciprocal."[269] The memoirist begins by listening deeply, and may be moved to write from perspectives that may surprise her. "Dialogue—in the ideal sense—necessitates both the capacity to deeply receive the other and the capacity to receive oneself; to allow the other a voice and to allow the self voice." [270] To undertake a conscious memoir is to begin a journey whose path is not known. The characters who come forward may have vantage points not seen or heard previously by the writer. If she is able to engage in imaginal dialogue, the story under construction will be more textured, more nuanced. "When the spontaneous dialogues of thought are approached from this point of view they flower into drama, poetry, or prayer. ...these dialogues reveal the complexity of thought as it struggles between perspectives, refusing to be simplified and narrowed to a single standpoint." [271]

Meeting the Ancestors

Just as imaginal psychology offers a way of conceptualizing and working with the Others in the self, it also offers a way to approach the ancestors. Memoir has long been a place for people to remember their ancestors, to tell their stories, to acknowledge their influence and the lessons of their lives. In Kingston's "No Name Woman" she explains the importance of naming and imagining her women ancestors because *"Unless I see her life branching into mine, she gives me no ancestral help."* [272] A memoirist knows her life is woven into the tapestry of those who came before her, even if the threads of their stories have been ripped away or damaged by lack of care. While the text she creates holds her stories, it can also re-weave the warp and woof of those who came before.

The ancestors are always present, and often, even more present by their very absence. It is often in the service of her ancestors, of the broken threads of their stories, that a woman undertakes a memoir. She becomes aware of how her ancestors' stories were or were not told and whether or not they were given proper tellings. Kingston acknowledges the paradox of bringing an ancestor's story forward; crafting a narrative may not offer the same solace to the ancestor that it offers the writer or reader. Upon concluding her re-telling of her nameless aunt, she writes:

> My aunt still haunts me—her ghost drawn to me because now, after fifty years of neglect, I alone devote pages of paper to her,… I do not think she always means me well. I am telling on her, and she was a spite suicide, drowning herself in the drinking water. The Chinese are always very frightened of the drowned one, whose weeping ghost, wet hair hanging and skin bloated, waits silently by the water to pull down a substitute. [273]

Crafting memoir can become a study of the "grateful dead." Folk tales with this motif emphasize honoring the dead and giving them proper burial, as David Miller suggests. [274] The point of such stories is, of course, that the ancestors require their due. For the writer of memoir, giving the ancestors their due may involve as little as keeping an apron or a photograph on one's writing desk, or as much as bringing their voice back through the vehicle of story. Writing the stories, especially those of trauma, becomes a way to honor those who were not able to speak for themselves. The stories that emerge are not only those of the writer's but those of a collective bloodline. Though the ghosts of the ancestors may be fundamentally ambivalent, the memoirist is aware that as a helpful ghost, an ancestor has power to inform and protect those who tend them.

According to scholar John Mbiti's explanation of the African concept of time, the ancestors are still considered part of the "sasa," the present flowing back to the divinities and God; it is only when they are no longer recollected by any living member of society that they pass into the ultimate ocean of time, the "zamani." [275] Mbiti chose to use these two words from Swahili to convey the concepts of past, present, and future. According to D.T. Naine, the word *sassa* in the Mande language refers to a hunter's bag which contain their personal fetishes.[276] In making associations to the Swahili *sasa* with the Mande *sassa*, one can see how ancestors are kept close to a person, much like the pouch that holds the objects of personal power. While they are still in a person's hunting bag, the fetishes are an interactive part of his/her reality. In the same way, to be able to recall one's ancestors keeps them in the long present (in one's pouch so to speak), where they can still encourage relationships with the living. Once they are forgotten, relationship is no longer possible and they pass on to the true "grave yard of time."

So many women have no stories of their foremothers, no literal narratives of their experiences. Instead, what is saved may include photographs, official certificates of birth or marriage, a box of postcards, a sewing basket, recipe cards. The fact that these objects remain is the only testimony to these women's value, because no one wrote down the experiences or events from which they emerged. Often what has been passed down has been a piece of jewelry, a quilt, or some other handcraft: Matter instead of Mother. Yet with the aid of the imaginal field, a photograph or a humble heirloom can become a portal to an ancestor's narrative. By studying it deeply one can begin to listen to "matter" for the stories it holds.

I have two gingham aprons, one turquoise and one blue, both are cross stitched. One with white thread the other with blue. The turquoise one was made by my great grandmother, Maude Lena, and the blue by my grandmother, Edna Margaret. Memories of my great grandmother Maude are scant. I can recall her tidy home that we visited only on special occasions, like Easter or her birthday. The surfaces were spotless, no dust or mussed edges in sight. Even her crocheted afghans were folded in precise rectangles and stacked neatly on the end of her sofa. She wore a hair net and severe black framed glasses. We had to be quiet, mindful of our hands and feet if we were to accompany my mother on these visits. I remember she kissed me on the cheek at my Aunt's wedding. I was in the receiving line wearing a new dropped-waist pink dress and black patent leather Mary-Janes, holding the basket of rice and feeling very excited to be a part of such a spectacle. Her skin was papery white and she smelled like lavender soap. "Don't you look so grown up?" Those are the only words I have of hers, the only event outside our visits to her house we shared. There was so much more to her life, but I wouldn't discover these things until I was well into my own adulthood and raising my own daughters.

I knew my own grandmother, Edna Margaret, to be a very shy person who lost her father while she was a young girl. Her poor self esteem, her willingness to live with the verbal and emotional abuse meted out by my grandfather, reverberated in my own mother. When I touch this apron, it reminds me of how confined my grandmother's life was, how afraid she was to stitch outside the neatly woven boxes of gingham. I am reminded of keeping up appearances, a cheerful little half apron, typical of the 1930s, a piece of fabric to be tied at the waist which had very little to do with really protecting one's clothes during domestic chores. It is a piece of female costume that bears witness to the happy face she put on despite personal tragedies. Her husband fell and broke his back while working in a ship yard during WWII. They had no money for a long hospitalization, so he recuperated at home while she got a job as a book keeper at a local college. She kept an immaculate house and presented an equally immaculate personal appearance. Her costume jewelry was always coordinated with her sensible but stylish clothing. I never saw her cry or get angry, though what she witnessed of my mother's life circumstances afforded her many opportunities.

Two aprons. Two lives. Two women who came before me and left ordinary needlework behind. Memories live in matter if we take the time to let them speak.

This idea of matter evoking the ancestors was part of Grace Lewis-McLaren's *The Mythos Quartet,* a work that demonstrates a woman's use of the imaginal to both construct and converse with her ancestor women. She examines three sets of journals: those of her mother, those of a great aunt, and those of her maternal grandmother. While each of these women left her words in the form of personal journals, there were still many unanswered questions about their lives, a sense that there was *more* to each of their stories than even their personal journals could explain. McLaren explored these journals imaginally, including artifacts, pictures, oral family stories, and her own personal experiences to compose a portrait of her motherline.[277] To balance out the similarities of class, race, and culture she discovered among the three women from her bloodline, she also includes her personal journey in the discovery of an imaginal ancestor from Africa. The weaving of this narrative is a beautiful demonstration of how one's motherline sings one into being.

McLaren comes from a line of women who valued the Divine song, sung in the tradition of Protestant Christianity, women who were strong in the face of adversity, who managed to live their lives with dignity despite the constraints of the culture and the dominant Christian myth. McLaren's personal story of being opened to the imaginal through a piece of sculpture and the subsequent journey to Africa echoes the same receptivity to the Divine Song, though now sung in the key of Zimbabwe. McLaren describes how the memory of another woman's culture and spirituality was evoked from the matter out of which it was carved, a memory that continues to nourish both the writer and her readers.

Like many writers, I keep mementos on my desk. Because I have been engaged in discovering my ancestor women through writing for the past ten years, I keep my grandmother's teacup and saucer, another grandmother's magnifying glass, two gingham aprons, bird feathers, a lacy dried leaf from a walk in the country, a silver turtle and crystal hand-warmer that belonged to my mother-in-law, and the mask of a dream figure whose face is pearly and decorated with

167

forget-me-nots and twigs of rosemary. These artifacts surround me as I write; they give me a sense of connection to both my literal and imaginal roots. Writer Kent Haruf has a similar experience with memories that live in matter and notes how such mementos also provide him symbols for what is mysterious and holy in his vocation of writing.

> ...having them makes a difference. I suppose in some way totemic. The things on my desk and on the walls above it connect me emotionally to memories, ways of living, people and geographical areas that are important to me. It's an emotional attachment to all these things that connects me up with the impulse to write....Every time I go down to work, I feel as if I'm descending into a sacred place. [278]

The intention of the memoirist is to call up events, people, and places, so it only makes sense that part of the ritual of a writer includes the presence of objects that represent the ancestors and those who are part of the writer's imaginal lineage. The ritual of collecting such material is in keeping with the Greek Goddess of Memory, Mnemosyne; as it is she who joins memories with matter, the stuff of our lives. The memoirist respects both substance and ephemera; both a grandmother's magnifying glass and the associations of her face, her laughter, her flour-smudged face while letting her granddaughter help bake a batch of sugar cookies. The memoirist senses the connectedness of her own story to all those with whom she shares a blood line and all those who have crossed her path. The objects we collect on the writing desk serve as ritual portals, places from which stories emerge, places from which stories can be evoked.

As a memoirist retrieves her stories, she becomes aware of the sacrifice of the ancestors and her own need to enact rituals of gratitude. The stories she writes are possible only because of her coming to this place in time by virtue of the ladders, both physical and imaginal, provided by those who preceded her. It is the memoirist who makes it possible for the voices of the ancestors to yet be heard in the contemporary moment and for the generations who will follow. While the stories of one's lineage can never be told in the literal words of the ancestors, the vehicle of memoir makes it possible to imagine their stories, to give them body and breath once more. The memoirist knows the importance of acknowledging the source of her imaginal gifts. My personal ritual of gratitude involves lighting a candle to recognize the presence of the ancestors as I write, and placing the first copy of work on my 'grandmother' altar when it is completed. Like Amy Tan, I am aware of the many voices who stand just behind me, each whispering from time to time: "Please, don't forget me." I like to imagine that my grandmothers, all my women, see their own words in mine. I like to imagine that they feel acknowledged and thanked, and that they witness my gratitude. Amy Tan Muses about the gifts of knowing the stories of her foremothers, of bringing the ancestors voices forward,

...Because I too have wondered why I can write about what I don't know. Yet I do know things. I have always known them, I realize. I've known them from my childhood, perhaps from listening to my mother and my aunties gossip about their secrets as they shelled the fava beans and pummeled the dumpling dough at the kitchen table. They spoke Shanghainese, a language I now, as an adult, cannot speak. I must have intuitively understood as a child. I must have paid close attention when their voices lowered and the rush of shameful words streamed out. How else is it I know their secrets? Or is it that I've known things because of all those suicidal threats my mother made when I was a child? I paid attention to her laments, what she said she wanted to forget. I've known things because we had to move so often, and I had a mother who believed happiness was a place she had never been. I've known things from listening to her talk about dangers of every form, unwanted babies, a man who will kiss you and ruin your life. She helped me imagine fully the unhappy consequences and all their gory details—what can happen if you don't have a mother to listen to. Today my mother is gone, but I still know certain things. They are in my bones. [279]

Mnemosyne and the Imaginal Field

As we come to the center of this set of nested circles, we find Mnemosyne. She is the figure who makes the imaginal field possible. Just as she is offspring of matter and air, the imaginal field is her creation, the offspring of physical experience and the ephemera of re-collected perceptions.

Mnemosyne inspires the writer to construct a narrative, a threshold to experience, and offers the reader possibilities of new perspectives. When reader meets writer, something new is created. The intersection of the reader's experiences with that of the text creates new perspectives and ways of beginning to understand an "other." The writer of memoir stands in a long imaginal lineage. One that from the time of the Greeks has been concerned with matter, ephemera, re-collection, and re-membering. With this image of Mnemosyne in the background, I have come to appreciate how the smallest fragments of a memory can unfold a story whose medicine I hadn't realized I needed until I wrote it down. As life would so instruct me, while I was engaged in my studies of metaphor and memory, my mother-in-law began her long descent into Alzheimer's. She gave me many lessons on the nature of memory and what we keep before we parted. Here is one of them.

....

These days when I open a drawer in the kitchen, I find myself lingering over placemats, napkins, dish towels, and pot holders. Like most people who have been married over two decades, our house is one with full closets, full drawers, full cupboards. There are too many placemats and napkins, many of them worn on the edges, colors fading, and fabric thinning. I can't quite bear to throw them away. Memories live here. My mother-in-law sewed beautifully in her day and when we were newly married, she delighted in adding to the stores of our home-in-the-making. I open the cupboard where we store the placemats, and memories fall out at my feet like so many squares of carefully stitched napkins.

Blues, creams, calico prints; fabric was her medium of expression. The dining room table, our place for family communion over the years, has been a place to nurture both body and soul. I love setting a cozy table, one with color and texture to set off a meal. Mom was happy to help.

I reach down and pick up a place mat that has spilled on the floor. It is one of the machine quilted ones, a log-cabin pattern. I close my eyes and recall handling the bolts of the cloth I'd chosen at the fabric store, carrying the arm sized bolts to the cutting table, and hearing the quiet scritch-scritch of the clerk's scissors as she cut the cloth I'd chosen for this set of place mats.

Mom was working on one of her ongoing craft projects, this time it was machine quilting. Shopping for fabric was a feminine ritual in which I had been happy to participate. I had learned how to sew in high school, though at the time my efforts were purely motivated by necessity for clothes that were less expensive that those from local department stores. My mother-in-law sewed for the joy of keeping herself occupied with the possibilities of creation. In some ways I suppose it was a distraction for her, a distraction from the now empty house.

I remember our first trip to a fabric store together, something a mother and daughter would do. This was a relationship I'd always wanted, a mother who was interested in my life and idiosyncrasies. From the time of my own parents divorce, my own mother seemed to slide into a black hole. I missed having a mom.

My mother-in-law missed female companionship too. She had several miscarriages before my husband was born, and had often said she had wanted more children. She raised a son, now she was getting a daughter. I was more than happy to be part of simple family rituals like making dinner together on family vacations.

She became the mother I never had in so many ways. Someone to shop with on vacations, someone to take walks with, someone to swap recipes with, but most of all, an older woman to confide in.

We went to find the fabric for my wedding dress. I had in mind a simple white eyelet. It was the December before Dave and I married. We had tried several places, but couldn't find the eyelet I wanted until the last store. It was candle light white with single eyelet flowers scattered through the fabric, perfect for the gown I envisioned. It was Mom who introduced me to the dressmaker, Mom who watched the fittings, Mom who eventually took the pictures of me modeling the finished gown, my hand holding the hem and laughing in delight.

I realize my heart is as full as my kitchen cupboards. Memories of Mom are embedded in the daily stuff of our lives, place mats, napkins, aprons. "Matter," "mater," "mother." Matter holds memory, gives it a place to live. Memories fill up our closets and spill out the doors. These days Mom is unraveling. She has Alzheimer's Disease. We take her objects and pictures in hopes of retrieving a momentary recognition, a remembrance of a past event that will light her face with a look of who she once was. Our rituals now are conversations of over-learned give-and-take, and sometimes there are small glimpses of who she used to be.

My heart is full to overflowing. My memories are both a comfort and a grief; such are the gifts of midlife.

....

It is I, Mnemosyne, that prompts your reverie. I live within your body, just as I lived within my mother's. Matter, mater, mother. I flit within your mind, like the breeze of my father sky. I am embedded in the stuff of life, and in the vague recognition of familiarity. I am both the earth and a vapor, my parent's child. I am Embodied Reverie, in matter and in spirit. I am here.

Appendix

Memory Muses Memoir Suggested Exercises

Below are the suggested exercises intended to engage modes of musing which are included in the text. I have found writing memoir a very healing endeavor. Mnemosyne lives all around us; she is embedded in the very stuff of our lives. Her daughters the Muses offer us many ways to enter, frame, shape, and shift the stories of our lives. There may be one Muse who steps forward, or one who taps you on the shoulder and says, "remember me?" Start with those exercises and see where she takes you. Remember, every story will carry the iridescence of many perspectives. These exercises are offered as stepping stones as you begin to re-collect and structure your life stories. I hope you enjoy the process and find what you need as you court Memory and her daughters.

1. Mnemosyne: Memories live in Matter

- Think of a treasured/ordinary object; if possible, hold it in your hands and study it for a few minutes. Why have you kept this object? What stories does it hold? If it could speak, what would it say?
- Ilene Beckerman has done a small sketch book titled *Love, Loss, and What I Wore* in which she explores the memories of pieces of clothing and the stories they each hold/evoke.
- Try this for yourself. Make a line drawing of a piece of clothing or an outfit from a particular period of your life. Write about it; why was it significant? What about it is clear/fuzzy in your mind now? What happened to it?
- Open a desk/kitchen/dresser drawer; list the objects you find. What stories live here, juxtaposed with one another?

2. Senses and Reveries

Try engaging Mnemosyne with your own senses. Our senses can often trigger powerful memories. Try it for yourself by completing each of the following phrases:

With the sight of …
With the sound of…
With the taste of…
With the scent of…
With the touch of…

Now write a page on each. If you discover you have more, keep going!

3. Myth Questions

Take a moment and answer Murdock's questions of 'mythic themes'. Try writing two pages per prompt. If you have more, keep going!

- *Who am I?* : List ten qualities that best describe you. Think of yourself at various ages 5, 10, 15, 21, your current age… Have you been aware of these qualities all along or have specific experiences/circumstances brought them forward? Which of your qualities is the most public/known to others? Which is the most private/least known? Which is the quality you couldn't you live without?
- *How do I make my way?* : List a few pivotal moments in your youth/young adulthood that set you on your current path in life. How did/do you support yourself? Who were/ are your closest friends and allies? Who were/are your enemies?
- *Who is my tribe?* : Describe your family of origin. What geographical location do you most identify with? Is there a line of work, study, or career choice that winds through family generations? Do you strongly identify with those who have preceded you or do see yourself as a maverick or aberration?
- *Why am I here?* : How do you answer this question for yourself? Does this question even matter to you? Do you rely

on institutions or particular communities to help answer this? Is there something you want to pass on to those who will follow? What do you want to be remembered for and why.

4. Content Exercises:

* Make a list of the events, people, places that have been important in your life.
* Start with ten, try to expand it to twenty, then thirty items.
* What has been your 'bottom line' when it has come to choosing which path to follow?
* Do you see any patterns, cycles, or nested boxes?
* How would you describe your own 'window' on the world?
* How has geography, family, friendships, and group affiliation influenced your life?
* Complete the phrase:

    "I have always…." Write two pages.

    "I have never…." Write two pages.

5. Form Exercises:

* Pick a moment from your life after which you knew things would never be the same. Try writing it 'straight', what are the facts; the who, what, when, where, why and how of it. Write it in the third person. Write it as an entry for a 'News About Town/Social Scene' section of the local newspaper.
* Take the same event and try writing it 'slant.' What do you imagine it looked like from the perspective of an onlooker? What effect did this experience have on your life? What do you want others to know about it? Why is it important to tell this story?
* Now try writing it 'messy.' Include as many sensory details as you can. What were the emotions of the situation? Use dialogue. Try to let the scene speak for itself.

6. Use Exercises:

* Answer the questions Audre Lourde poses: "What are the words you do not have yet? What do you need to say?"
* Why do you want to write?
* What is it you hope to accomplish?
* With whom do you hope to share your stories?

7. Reflection Exercise:

* Have you read a memoir of a person from a different place on the planet or a different culture than your own? Were you offered a threshold? What did you learn? What surprised you? Did you recognize parts of yourself?
* Whose stories have you read in which you have found overlapping parts of your own?

8. Mirror exercises:

* Do you have any memories of specific mirrors as you were growing up?
* Did you ever break a mirror? What happened?
* Are there particular surfaces that set you into reverie? What are they?
* What are your personal experiences with each of these kinds of mirrors…is one more interesting to you that the others? Why?

9. Mnemosyne's Touch: Multiplicity of Forms

Exercises in Perspective shifts

* Write out a pivotal moment, a time when something important happened, a time after which you knew things would never be quite the same again. Write it with the 5 W's— just the facts.
  * Now write it in third person, or as "once upon a time…", or from the first person perspective of

another person or object involved in the story

- an early memory: write it from the vantage point of scent and texture; now write it from sight and sound…now write it from taste
- your first pet; from your point of view, then the pet's point of view
- your favorite food as a child; from your point of view, then the point of view of the one who prepared the food or the venue who served it…

10. Clio: "History, events as they occurred"

- Create a personal history list:
- Begin with your birth and continue by creating a list of all your life's important events and relationships. Your list can have hundreds of items. When you sit down to write a story, you'll have this list of topics handy. The list helps you to focus on things that deserve the most attention. It also primes the pump of memory: the more you write, the more you'll remember. At first just jot things down. As the list gets longer, organize it chronologically. With your list, you will always have a place to go for your next piece of writing.

Now choose ten items that you feel were the most formative. Select one and write the event as succinctly as you can, use the 5 W's.

- Re-write it as a narrative, use 'softer eyes'.
- Try writing it in the third person.
- Look through a scrapbook… your photo collection or a high school year book…select an image of yourself and write a story of that day. Let one picture catch your eye or allow a succession of images provide insight into someone's development or decline. Let these images inspire you to write –about the time, incidents, or emotions the photographs evoke. You may notice a pattern in the photos you have saved. What images have you chosen to keep? Notice the changes wrought by age and fashion. What do these photos say about the people

who shot them? What do they say about the times when they were taken? Pay attention to what is not in the picture as well as what sits in the periphery. If you are writing about another time and place, you will find old picture books a valuable resource. Look carefully at the hairstyles, the clothing, the props.

* Try looking through the daily newspaper; the want ads, the obituaries, the business section, the sports or local events. Notice which articles grab your attention, what they remind you of. You may find a bit of personal history gets jogged, write it down!

* Is there someone form your past that you would like to write a letter? A friend? A teacher? A former spouse? Try writing to them and say what you were never able to tell this person. Share some of the insights you've gained since your last communication. You need not mail this letter—simply voice your thoughts and feelings on paper. You may come to understand an unresolved issue that has blocked your progress or haunted one of your recollections.

* Create a background file on one of the characters in your memoir. Try Ira Progoff's Stepping Stones technique— imagine the twelve most significant events in a relative's life starting with birth and ending with the present moment. ...try to imagine his/her history, the daily details of their life. How many children, if any, did this person have? Where did he/she work? Was there a major crisis in this person's life? Look for clues in your subject's dress, location, and demeanor. Develop several different scenarios, how might this particular story have unfolded? You can interpret character to mean place, invention, or institution. Imagine the people who occupied a house over several generations. Picture the dramas that occurred in various rooms. What was the neighborhood like when the house was first built?

11. Calliope: "Hero stories, epic stories, poetic stories"

* write about a time you met a hero, or were a hero to someone else

- visit your personal history list; create an epic poem of that captures a portion of your life or an epic poem that honors your roots or heritage.
- review your personal history list; write three poems;
    - one to capture a precious past moment
    - the second to capture the love of a friend
    - the third to capture a powerful turning point in your life.

Play around with titles for each entry on your personal history list. Just brainstorm, don't censor your ideas. Don't be afraid to be silly. Try looking through a book of quotations or poetry for ideas. Create a list of chapter titles to guide you through and extended piece of writing.

- Epics are driven by strong emotion; fear, love, hate. Every human being has experiences with these emotions.
- Think about someone from your personal history list… (or if you are fearless, yourself)…what is this person afraid of? In love with? What does he/she loathe?
- …Think back to a terrifying moment in your life—a car accident, a walk down an unlit street, a situation in which you were almost caught doing something wrong—describe the physical sensations you experienced. Write down the thoughts that went through your head at the time. Record any delayed reactions you had as well.
    - …Take a few minutes to think about something that terrified you when you were little. Write it from a child's point of view.

12. Polyhymnia: "Stories of reverence, of pauses, of Ritual"

- Describe an 'a-ha' moment of connection to something beyond yourself
- Describe a place that sets you to reverie…

- Write about an experience of solitude…
- Write about the first time you ever saw a mime performance
- Work the experience of sounds into your writing. Revisit an episode from your personal history list. Take a minute to imagine what sounds might be going on in the background. Are there voices in the distance? Can you hear laughter? Crying? Whispering? Arguing? Are there any machines you can hear? A refrigerator humming? The bell of a cash register? The music or static coming from a radio or a particular T.V. program? Try to weave ore sounds into your work.

Create a Sacred Space for writing. Make your workspace into an altar, a sacred place where ideas and archetypes can act out their dramas. Put pictures of loved ones on your desk. Place a flower in a vase or an object of beauty in your sight line. ... Your desk need not be neat—it need not be a desk at all—but make it a sacred spot that will entice your Muse to visit.

13. Melpomene: "Grief stories"

- Write about a loss…first awareness of mortality… disappointment with an important person…a deep personal wound…
- Write about your sources of comfort/inspiration during difficult times
- …a story of forgiveness…
- …a story of compassion in response to tragedy…
- …read the obituaries, find a story, write a eulogy for a real or fictional character
- …think about your relationship to rituals. Rituals separate time, set boundaries so that when it is time to work, we can really focus and when it is time to celebrate or mourn, we can do so fully. Rituals help us shift gears, make transitions, change our mental states.

…Each of us has rituals for getting up in the morning and going to bed each night, but we often don't notice the details of our own behavior. Practice mindfulness. Just how do you brush your teeth and wash your face? Are there any rituals from your personal history list that stand out? Birth stories? Religious rituals? Funerals/ Memorials?

14. Terpsichore: "Dance, body stories"

- Write about the first time you remember dancing...
- Write about a time you saw your parents dance...
- Describe your relationship to movement...have you ever had dance lessons?
- The first time you saw a dance performance...ballet... modern...ethnic...
- Your awareness of the variety of rhythms and what each calls out of your body...
- Your experience with sports...exercise...gym class...yoga... *Think about this quote from the movie, Chariots of Fire, "...when I run, I feel His pleasure." Describe a moment when participating in movement of your body connected you to something larger than yourself*

15. Thalia: "Comedy, community stories"

- a funny story from your childhood...
- a family incident that is retold over and over because it makes people laugh
- a favorite comedian...
- a favorite comic strip...
- a favorite play/movie ...are there particular scenes that make you laugh each time you see them?
- A time when laughter shifted a tension...
- A time when laughter wasn't expected, but helped weave a sense of community in the moment...
- Family jokes...knock-knock jokes...why did the x cross the street jokes...

Find a book to use for inspiration. Pick a page at random from an atlas and write a poem about that place. Open an encyclopedia and write a love song mentioning the first topic on the left-hand page. Pull a name from the phone book and write a description of that person's living room. None of this has to be for publication, it is simply a way to get loosened up and have a little fun.

16. Euterpe: "Breath stories, music stories"

- listen to your favorite music…what images emerge?
- Do you remember a piece of music from your childhood? Was it a lullaby? A song? Instrumental? Can you close you eyes and hear it now? What feelings does it evoke?
- Write a story of a time a piece of music touched you deeply
- Write a story of the role of music in your family of origin…If you play/ed a musical instrument/sing; write about the process of learning; Who was your teacher? When did you perform? What kept you going? Is there a particular performance that stands out in your memory?

17. Urania: "Dream stories, Star stories"

- 'what lies above and beyond also lies within'…Write a description of a place in nature and reflect how it speaks to you…
- Write a story of star gazing…first time you recognized a constellation…
- Write a story of wonder in the face of a natural phenomenon…
- Write a dream story…your first awareness of dreams…your relationship to dreams, do you write them down? Your last dream, your association to its images…
- Write a revelation of something Sacred

18. Erato: "Love Stories"

- Write a story of a 'first' love
- Write a story of 'brotherly-sisterly' love
- Write a story of 'sensual' love
- Write an experience of 'unconditional' love…

- Who were 'teachers of your heart'? How would you describe their lessons to you? How are those lessons present in your life today?
- What is your favorite love story/ romantic movie? How does this story parallel (or not!) your own experience of love?
- Tristine Rainer, author of *Your Life as Story*, suggests that, it memoir as well as fiction, motivation must be a constant element: "The character [you] should have a clear desire line. It can bend, it can turn unexpectedly, but it should not break. It should be intense and continuous. As soon as one need is met, another appears." Map out your own 'desire' line on a piece of paper. Look at the places where it changes from desire for a relationship to desire for a particular relationship, then to desiring what comes next.... The complications of formal commitment, or not (!) Jot down the incidents that illustrate the various stages of desire as they are challenged by conflicting needs or circumstances.
- Engage your sense of scent. Think about the smells you associate with a loved one. Let the memory of this fragrance inspire you to write. Make a list of twenty-five smells—pleasant and unpleasant, natural and industrial. Choose one as a writing catalyst and let it trigger images, thoughts, and feelings. Go into your kitchen and smell some spices. Visit the bathroom and open some jars.

For Further Reading:

Arrien, Angeles. *The Nine Muses: A Mythological Path to Creativity.* New York: Jeremy P. Tarcher/Putnam, 2000.

Barrington, Judith. *Writing the Memoir: From Truth to Art.* Portland, OR: The Eighth Mountain Press, 1997.

Buss, Helen M. *Repossessing the World: Reading Memoirs by Contemporary Women.* Toronto, Ontario: Wilfrid Laurier University Press, 2002.

Campbell, Joseph. *Myths to Live By.* New York: Viking Penguin, 1972.

Conway, Jill Ker. *When Memory Speaks: Reflections on Autobiography.* New York: Knopf, 1998.

DeSalvo, Louise. *Writing as a Way of Healing: How Telling Our Stories Transforms Our Lives.* Boston: Beacon Press, 1999.

Eakin, Paul John. *How Our Lives Become Stories: Making Selves.* Ithaca: Cornell U P, 1999.

Goldberg, Natalie. *Writing Down the Bones.* Boston: Shambhala, 2005.

Hampl, Patricia. *I Could Tell You Stories.* New York: Norton, 1999.

Hillman, James. *The Myth of Analysis.* New York: Harper Perennial, 1992.

—. *Healing Fiction.* Woodstock, Connecticut: Spring Publications, 1983.

—. *Re-Visioning Psychology.* New York: Harper & Row, 1975.

Hollis, James. *Tracking the Gods: The Place of Myth in Modern Life.* Toronto: Inner City Books, 1995.

Lepore, Stephen. *The Writing Cure: How Expressive Writing Promotes Health and Emotional Well-Being.* New York: American Psychological Association, 2002.

Metzger, Deena. *Writing for Your Life: A Guide and Companion to the Inner Worlds.* New York: HarperSanFrancisco, 1992.

Murdock, Maureen. *The Heroine's Journey.* Boston: Shambhala, 1990.

—. "Telling Our Stories: Making Meaning from Myth and Memoir." *Depth Psychology: Meditations in the Field.* Ed. Dennis Patrick Slattery and Lionel Corbett. Einsiedeln, Switzerland: Daimon Verlag, 2000. 129-139.

—. *Unreliable Truth: On Memoir and Memory.* New York: Seal Press, 2003.

Paris, Ginette. *Pagan Grace.* Woodstock, CT. Spring Publications, 1990.

—. *Pagan Meditations.* Woodstock, CT. Spring Publications, 1997.

Pennebaker, James W. *Opening Up: The Healing Power of Confiding in Others.* New York: William Morrow, 1990.

—. *Writing to Heal: A Guided Journal for Recovering from Trauma and Emotional Upheaval.* Oakland, CA: New Harbinger Publications, Inc., 2004.

Romanyshyn, Robert D. *Mirror and Metaphor: Images and Stories of Psychological Life.* Pittsburg, PA: Trivium Publications, 2001.

Tan, Amy. *The Opposite of Fate: Memories of a Writing Life.* New York: Penguin Books, 2003.

Ueland, Brenda. *Me: A Memoir.* Duluth, Minnesota: Holy Cow! Press, 1994.

Zimmerman, Susan. *Writing to Heal the Soul: Transforming Grief and Loss Through Writing.* New York, NY: Three Rivers Press, 2002.

Zinsser, William. *Inventing the Truth: The Art and Craft of Memoir.* Boston: Mariner Books, 1998.

Sources:

(Endnotes)

1   Downing, Christine. 26. *The Goddess: Mythological Images of the Feminine* (New York: The Crossroad Publishing Company, 1984).

2   Maureen Murdock, *Monday Morning Memoirs* (United States: Xlibris, 2002),13.

3   Ovid, *The Metamorphoses,* Book Six, line 114.

4   Norman Shine, "Counting on the Future: The Art and Science of Numerology." *The World Atlas of Divination* (Boston: Bullfinch Press, 1992), 190.

5   Ginette Paris, *Pagan Grace* (Woodstock, Connecticut: Spring, 1990), 121.

6   Hesiod, *Theogony, Works and Days, Shield* Trans. Apostolos N. Athanassakis (Baltimore: The John Hopkins U P, 1983), 917.

7   John Carey, "The Daughters of Memory." *Temenos,* 7 (1986) 226-27.

8   Suzette Henke, *Shattered Subjects: Trauma and Testimony in Women's Life Writing* .(New York: St. Martin's, 2000), 187.

9   William Zinsser, *Inventing the Truth: The Art and Craft of Memoir* (Boston: Mariner Books, 1998), 3.

10 Charles Baxter, "Shame and Forgetting in the Information Age," *The Business of Memory*. (Saint Paul, MN: Graywolf Press, 1999), ix.

11 Patricia Hampl, *I Could Tell You Stories* (New York: Norton, 1999), 35.

12 Allen Mandelbaum, trans. *The Metamorphoses of Ovid* (New York: Harcourt, 1993), 91.

13 Patricia Hampl, "Memory and Imagination." *The Anatomy of Memory*, Ed. James McConkey (New York: Oxford UP, 1996), 210.

14 Dena Metzger, *Writing for Your Life: A Guide to Writing Memoir* (New York: HarperSanFrancisco, 1992),33.

15 Judith Barrington, *Writing Memoir: From Truth to Art*. (Portland, OR: The Eighth Mountain Press, 1997), 29.

16 Patricia Hampl, *I Could Tell You Stories* (New York :Norton, 1999), 29.

17 James Hillman, *Healing Fiction* (Woodstock, CT: Spring, 1983), 40-42

18 James Hillman, *Healing Fiction* (Woodstock, CT: Spring, 1983), 43.

19 Thomas Hale, *Griots and Griottes: Masters of Word and Music* (Bloomington: Indiana Press, 1998), 24.

20 James Hillman, *Healing Fiction* (Woodstock, CT: Spring, 1983), 49.

21 Maureen Murdock, "Telling Our Stories," *Depth Psychology: Meditations in the Field*. Ed. Dennis Patrick Slattery and Lionel Corbett. Einsiedeln, Switzerland: Daimon Verlag, 2000), 133.

22 James Hollis, *Tracking the Gods: The Place of Myth in Modern Life,* (Toronto: Inner City Books, 1995), 21.

23 Maureen Murdock "Telling Our Stories," 137.

24 Maureen Murdock "Telling Our Stories 131.

25   Jill Kerr Conway, *When Memory Speaks: Reflections on Autobiography* (New York: Knopf, 1998),18.

26   Patricia Hampl, "Memory and Imagination," 208.

27   Sidonie Smith and Julia Watson, *Reading Autobiography: A guide for Interpreting Life Narratives*, (Minneapolis: U of Minnesota P, 2001), 1.

28   Sidonie Smith and Julia Watson, *Reading Autobiography,* 2.

29   Helen M. Buss, *Repossessing the World: Reading Memoirs by Contemporary Women* (Toronto, Ontario: Wilifrid Laurier UP, 2002), 11.

30   Helen M. Buss, *Repossessing the World: Reading Memoirs by Contemporary Women* (Toronto, Ontario: Wilifrid Laurier UP, 2002), 24.

31   Sidonie Smith and Julia Watson, *Reading Autobiography,* 3.

32   Sidonie Smith and Julia Watson, *Reading Autobiography,* 14.

33   Sidonie Smith and Julia Watson, *Reading Autobiography,* 11.

34   Janet Varner Gunn, *Autobiography: Toward a Poetics of Experience* (Philadelphia: U of Pennsylvania P, 1982), 8.

35   Lois Bloom and Margaret Lahey, *Language Development and Language Disorders* (New York: Wiley and Sons, 1978), 11.

36   Suzanne Juhasz, "Towards a Theory of Form in Feminist Autobiography: Kate Millet's *Flying* and *Sita*; Maxine Hong Kingston's *The Woman Warrior*." *Women's Autobiography: Essays in Criticism.* Ed. Estelle Jelinek. (Bloomington: Indiana U P, 1980), 223-24.

37   Patricia Berry, "What's the Matter with Mother?" *Echo's Subtle Body.* (Dallas, Texas: Spring, 1982), 1.

38   Richard G. Lillard, *American Autobiography: A Descriptive Guide* (Stanford: Stanford UP, 1956), 156.

39   Estelle C. Jelinek, *The Tradition of Women's Autobiography from Antiquity to the Present,* 188.

40   Claudine. Hermann, *The Tongue Snatchers.* Trans. Nancy Cline. Lincoln and London: U of Nebraska P, 1989. ix.

41   Helen Buss, *Repossessing the World,* 16.

42   *Repossessing the World* ,12.

43   Long, Judy. 37.

44   Claudine, Hermann, *The Tongue Snatchers.* 25.

45   Judy Long, *Telling Women's Lives,*37.

46   Judy Long, *Telling Women's Lives,*38.

47   Judy Long, 40.

48   Helen Buss, 186.

49   Kathleen. Dehler, "The Need to Tell All: A Comparison of Historical and Modern Feminist 'Confessional' Writing." *Feminist Criticism.* Eds. Cheryl Brown and Karen Olson. (Metuchen, New Jersey: The Scarecrow Press, 1978), 339.

50   Leigh Gilmore, *Autobiographics,* 40.

51   Leigh Gilmore, *Autobiographics,* 40.

52   Jeanne Perrault, *Writing Selves,* 7.

53   Jeanne Perrault, *Writing Selves,* 133-34.

54   Audre Lourde, quoted in Jeanne Perrault, *Writing Selves,* 134.

55   Suzette Henke, *Shattered Subjects: Trauma and Testimony in Women's Life Writing.* (New York: St. Martin's, 2000), xii.

56   Alberto Manguel, *A History of Reading* (New York: Viking, 1996), 173.

57   Patricia Meyer Spacks, *The Female Imagination*, 241.

58   Elizabeth Spelman, *The Inessential Woman,* 179.

59   Melchoir-Bonnet, Sabine. *The Mirror: A History.* New York: Routledge, 2001.

60   Pendergrast, Mark. *Mirror, Mirror: A History of the Human Love Affair with Reflection.* New York: Basic Books, 2003.

61   Berger, John. *Ways of Seeing.* London: Penguin, 1977.

62   Trude McDermott, "The Red Dress Series." The Fresno Art Museum. Fresno, California, 1996.

63   David L Miller, "Foreword." in Robert D. Romanyshyn, *Mirror and Metaphor: Images and Stories of Psychological Life.* Pittsburg, PA: Trivium Publications, 2001. xii-xvi.

64   Robert D. Romanyshyn, *Mirror and Metaphor: Images and Stories of Psychological Life.* Pittsburgh, Pennsylvania: Trivium Publications, 2001. 9.

65   Robert D. Romanyshyn, *Mirror and Metaphor ,* 11.

66   Lillian. Hellman, *Three: An Unfinished Woman, Pentimento, Scoundrel Time.* Boston: Little, Brown and Co., 1979. 309.

67   David L Miller. "Through a Looking Glass —The World as Enigma." *Eranos* 55: 1986. 371.

68   Gaston Bachelard, *Water and Dreams*. Trans. Edith R. Farrell. (Dallas, Texas: The Dallas Institute Publications, 1982), 21-24.

69   Pendergrast, 3.

70   Miller, D.L. "Through a Looking Glass —The World as Enigma." *Eranos* 55: 1986. 375.

71   Miller, D.L. "Through a Looking Glass. 375.

72   Pendergrast, 157.

73   Lynda Sexson, *Ordinarily Sacred.* 3.

74   Lynda Sexson, *Ordinarily Sacred.* 3.

75   Pendergrast, 15-16.

76   Miller, "Through a Looking Glass —The World as Enigma." *Eranos* 55: 1986. 375.

77   Miller, "Through a Looking Glass", 377.

78   Miller, "Through a Looking Glass" , 380.

79   Wolfgang Zucker, "Reflections on Reflection" *Journal of Aesthetics and Art Criticism* 20/3(1969):248-9.

80   Zucker "Reflections on Reflection" 248-9.

81   Lucien Dallenbach, *The Mirror in the Text.* Trans. J.Whitely and E. Hughes. (Chicago: U Chicago P, 1989), 35.

82   Miller, "Through a Looking Glass —The World as Enigma." *Eranos* 55: 1986. 399-401.

83   J. Hillis. Miller, *Ariadne's Thread: Story Lines.* (New Haven and London: Yale U P, 1992), 224.

84   Mieke Bal, "Mirrors of Nature." *Quoting Carrravggio: Contemporary Art, Preposterous History.* (Chicago: U Chicago P, 1999), 261.

85   Miller," Through a Looking Glass —The World as Enigma." *Eranos* 55: 1986. 402.

86   Gilles Deleuze, *The Logic of Sense.* Trans. M. Lester and C. Stivale. (New York: Columbia UP, 1990), 262.

87   Timothy Gantz, *Early Greek Myth: A Guide to Literary and Artistic Sources, Volume One* (Baltimore, Johns Hopkins UP, 1993), 55.

88   Gail Thomas" Pegasus." *The Muses.* Ed.Gail Thomas. (Dallas: The Dallas Institute Publications, 1994), 6.

89   Angeles Arrien, *The Nine Muses: A Mythological Path to Creativity* (New York: Jeremy P. Tarcher/Putnam, 2000), 14-15.

90   Barbara Hort, "The Sacred Story and the Divine Hush: Adventures in Polyhymnia's Wonderland." *Spring 70,* 2004.151.

91   Eileen Gregory. "Clio: Muse of History—"Things As They Are"." in *The Muses.* Ed. by Gail Thomas. (Dallas: The Dallas Institute Publications, 1994), 118.

92   Eileen Gregory. "Clio: Muse of History," 122.

93   Helen M Buss, *Repossessing the World: Reading Memoirs by Contemporary Women.* (Toronto, Ontario: Wilifrid Laurier University Press, 2002. xiv.

94   Angeles Arrien, *The Nine Muses* 37.

95   Dona S. Gower, "Calliope." in *The Muses.* Ed. by Gail Thomas. (Dallas: The Dallas Institute Publications, 1994), 111.

96   June Singer, qtd. In Feinstein, David and Stanley Krippner. *The Mythic Path.* (New York: G.P. Putnam's Sons, 1997), xvi-xvii.

97   Moss, Barbara Robinette. *Change Me into Zeus's Daughter.*(New York: Scribner, 2001).

98   Barbara Hort. "The Sacred Story and the Divine Hush: Adventures in Polyhymnia's Wonderland." *Spring 70,* 2004. 152-156.

99   Gaston Bachelard. *Water and Dreams.* Edith R. Farrell. Dallas, (Texas: The Dallas Institute Publications, 1982),15.

100 Gaston Bachelard. *Water and Dreams*, 195.

101 Daniel Russ, "Polyhymnia: The Creative Creature, Veiled and Pensive." in *The Muses.* Ed. by Gail Thomas. (Dallas: The Dallas Institute Publications, 1994), 21.

102 Angeles Arrien, 107.

103 Barbara Hort, 161.

104 Barbara Hort, 162.

105 Natalie Goldberg. *A Long Quiet Highway.* ix.

106 Natalie Goldberg. *A Long Quiet Highway.* ix.

107 Aurora Levins Morales. *Medicine Stories: History, Culture and the Politics of Integrity.* (Cambridge, MA: South End Press, 1998), 19.

108 Aurora Levins Morales. *Medicine Stories*, 20.

109 Carrin Dunne. "The Roots of Memory" in *Spring: A Journal of Archetype and Culture.* Dallas:Spring Publications, 1988. 48:114-15.

110 Brown, Laura. "Not Outside the Range: one Feminist Perspective on Psychic Trauma" in *Trauma: Explorations in Memory.* ed. Cathy Caruth. Baltimore: Johns Hopkins U P, 1995. 110.

111 Louise DeSalvo. *Writing as a Way of Healing.* 43.

112 Bessel van der Kolk and van der Hart. "The Intrusive Past: The Flexibility of Memory and the Engraving of Trauma" in *Trauma: Explorations in Memory.* ed. Cathy Caruth. Baltimore: Johns Hopkins U P, 1995. 178.

113 Louise DeSalvo, 6.

114 Marion Woodman, *Conscious Femininity.* (Toronto: Inner City Books, 1993), 136.

115 Adrienne Rich, "Notes on a Politics of Location." in *Arts of the Possible.* (New York: Norton, 2001), 211.

116 Dennis Slattery *The Wounded Body Remembering the Markings of Flesh.* (Albany: SUNY P, 2000), 19.

117 Dennis Slattery. *The Wounded Body,* 97.

118 Woodman, Marion. *Bone; Dying Into Life.*

119 Mary Lou Hoyle, "Thalia" in *The Muses.* Ed. Gail Thomas.(Dallas: The Dallas Institute Publications, 1994), 103.

120 Hoyle, "Thalia" 105-06.

121 Tristine Rainer, *Your Life as Story.*(NewYork, Tarcher, 1998), 289.

122 Ian Frasier. http://www.newyorker.com/reporting/2008/05/26/080526fa_ fact_frazier New Yorker online May 26 2008. http://blog.writersdigest. com/writersperspective/Ian+Frazier+On+Humor+Writing.aspx.

123 www.theoi.com.

124 Robert S. Dupree. "Euterpe: Muse of the Saxophone." in *The Muses.* Ed. by Gail Thomas. (Dallas: The Dallas Institute Publications, 1994), 54.

125 Robert S. Dupree. "Euterpe: Muse of the Saxophone", Andrew Barker qtd, 60.

126 Robert S. Dupree. "Euterpe: Muse of the Saxophone", Victor Zuckerkandl qtd. 68.

127 Darcy Woodall, "Urania: Transcendent Muse." *Spring 70,* 2004.168.

128 Robert Sardello, "Urania." in *The Muses.* Ed. by Gail Thomas. (Dallas: The Dallas Institute Publications, 1994), 12.

129 Sardello, "Urania." 13.

130 Sardello, "Urania." 16.

131 Fredrick Turner, "Erato" in *The Muses.* Ed. Gail Thomas. (Dallas: The Dallas Institute Publications, 1994), 37.

132 Angeles Arrien. 65.

133 Angeles Arrien. 65.

134 Fredrick Turner. "Erato" 38.

135 Fredrick Turner "Erato" 39-40.

136 Robert S. Dupree, "Euterpe: Muse of the Saxophone." in *The Muses.* Ed. by Gail Thomas.(Dallas: The Dallas Institute Publications, 1994),71.

137 Derrick Jensen, "A Weakened World Cannot Forgive Us" An Interview With Kathleen Dean Moore *The Sun,* March 2001: 5

138 May Sarton, *Recovering: A Journal 1978-79.*

139 Louise De Salvo, *Writing as a Way of Healing.*

140 Lois Bloom and Margaret Lahey. *Language Development and Language Disorders.* (New York: Wiley and Sons, 1978), 15.

141 Farrah Jasmine Griffiths, "Textual Healing: Claiming Black Women's Bodies, the Erotic and Resistance in Contemporary Novels of Slavery." 2001. Online. 17.

142 Judith Lewis Herman, *Trauma and Recovery.*(New York: Harper Collins, 1992), 51.

143 Cathy Caruth, *Trauma: Explorations in Memory.* (Baltimore: John Hopkins University Press, 1995) 4-5.

144 Caruth, *Trauma,* 4-5.

145 Caruth, *Trauma,* 4-5.

146 Judith Lewis Herman, *Trauma and Recovery.* (New York: Harper Collins, 1992), 37.

147 Bessel A. Van der Kolk, "The Body Keeps Score: Approaches to the Psycho-biology of Posttraumatic Stress Disorder." in Van der Kolk, Besssel A., Alexander McFarlane, Lars Weisaeth, eds. *Traumatic Stress: The Effects of Overwhelming Experience on Mind, Body, and Society.*(New York: The Guilford Press, 1996), 3.

148 Caruth, *Trauma,* 6.

149 Dori Laub, "Bearing Witness or the Vicissitudes of Listening" in *Testimony: Crisis of Witnessing in Literature, Psychoanalysis, and History.* Shoshana Felman and Dori Laub, M.D. New York: Routledge, 1992. 57.

150 Dori Laub, "Truth and Testimony: The Process and the Struggle" in *Trauma: Explorations in Memory.* Ed. Cathy Caruth. (Baltimore: John Hopkins U P, 1995), 68.

151 Caruth, *Trauma,* 7.

152 Caruth, *Trauma* 7.

153 Emily Dickinson, *The Complete Collected Poetry of Emily Dickinson.* New York: Little, Brown and Company, 1980. 294.

154 Caruth, *Trauma* 10.

155 Caruth, *Trauma* 11.

156 Bessel A., Van der Kolk, and Onno Van Der Hart. "The Intrusive Past: The Flexibility of Memory and the Engraving of Trauma" in *Trauma: Explorations in Memory.* ed. Cathy Caruth. Baltimore: Johns Hopkins U P, 1995.159.

157 Henri Ellenberger *The History of the Unconscious.* (New York: Basic Books, 1970), 272-3.

158 Bessel A. Van der Kolk and Onno Van Der Hart. "The Intrusive Past: The Flexibility of Memory and the Engraving of Trauma" in *Trauma: Explorations in Memory.* ed. Cathy Caruth. (Baltimore: Johns Hopkins U P, 1995, 158-9.

159 Henri Ellenberger. *The History of the Unconscious.* New York: Basic Books, 1970. 373.

160 Bessel A. Van der Kolk and Onno Van Der Hart. "The Intrusive Past: The Flexibility of Memory and the Engraving of Trauma" in *Trauma: Explorations in Memory.* ed. Cathy Caruth (Baltimore: Johns Hopkins U P, 1995), 164.

161 Bessel A. Van der Kolk and Onno Van Der Hart. "The Intrusive Past: The Flexibility of Memory and the Engraving of Trauma" in *Trauma: Explorations in Memory.* ed. Cathy Caruth. (Baltimore: Johns Hopkins U P, 1995), 164.

162 Bessel A. Van der Kolk, R. Blitz, W.A.Burr, and E. Hartmann."Nightmares and Trauma: Life-long and traumatic Nightmares in Veterans." *American Journal of Psychiatry* 141: 187-190. 1984.

163 Marion Woodman, *Conscious Femininity.* (Toronto: Inner City Books, 1993),136.

164 Babette Rothschild, *The Body Remembers.* (New York: W.W. Norton, 2000),xiv.

165 Bessel A. Van der Kolk, and Onno Van Der Hart. "The Intrusive Past: The Flexibility of Memory and the Engraving of Trauma" in *Trauma* 176.

166 Bessel A. Van der Kolk, and Onno Van Der Hart. "The Intrusive Past: The Flexibility of Memory and the Engraving of Trauma" in *Trauma*

167 Andrew Brink, *Creativity as Repair.* London: Cromleck Press,1982. 1.

168 Alice Sebold. *Lucky.* (New York: Scribner, 1999), 33.

169 Louise DeSalvo. *Writing as a Way of Healing: How Telling Our Stories Transforms Our Lives.* (Boston: Beacon Press, 1999), 43.

170 Bessel A. Van der Kolk and Onno Van Der Hart. "The Intrusive Past." 178.

171 Mark Doty. *Heaven's Coast: A Memoir.* (New York: HarperPerennial,1996), ix.

172 Louise DeSalvo. *Writing as a Way of Healing.* 6.

173 Suzette A.Henke, *Shattered Subjects Trauma and Testimony in Women's Life Writing.* (New York: St.Martin's, 2000), xi.

174 Louise DeSalvo. *Writing as a Way of Healing* 11.

175 Louise DeSalvo. *Writing as a Way of Healing* 12.

176 Judith Lewis Herman. *Trauma and Recovery.*(New York: Harper Collins, 1992), 183.

177 Judith Lewis Herman. *Trauma and Recovery.*(New York: Harper Collins, 1992), 183.

178 Judith Lewis Herman. *Trauma and Recovery.* New York: Harper Collins, 1992. 181.

179 Suzette Henke, *Trauma and Testimony in Women's Life Writing.* (New York: St.Martin's, 2000), xxii.

180 Alice Walker. "Saving the Life That Is Your Own: The Importance of Model's in the Artist's Life." in *In Search of Our Mother's Gardens.* (New York: Harcourt Brace Jovanovich, 1983), 14.

181 James Hillman. *Healing Fiction.* Woodstock, Connecticut: Spring Publications, 1983. 3-4.

182 James Hillman. *Healing Fiction.* 42-3.

183 James Hillman. *Healing Fiction.* 42-3.

184 James Hillman. *Healing Fiction.* 7.

185 James Hillman. *Healing Fiction.* 7.

186 James Hillman. *Healing Fiction.* 19.

187 James Hillman. *Healing Fiction.* 8.

188 James Hillman. *Healing Fiction.* 9.

189 James Hillman. *Healing Fiction.* 9.

190 James Hillman. *Healing Fiction.* 12.

191 James Hillman. *Healing Fiction.* 12.

192 James Hillman. *Healing Fiction.* 23.

193 James Hillman. *Healing Fiction.* 41.

194 Maureen Murdock. *Unreliable Truth: On Memoir and Memory.* (New York: Seal Press, 2003), 75.

195 Louise DeSalvo. *Writing as a Way of Healing.* 176.

196 James Hillman, *Healing Fiction.* 43-44.

197 James Hillman, *Healing Fiction.* 44.

198 James Hillman, *Healing Fiction.* 45.

199 James Hillman, *Healing Fiction.* 46.

200 Qtd in Louise DeSalvo, *Writing as a Way of Healing: How Telling Our Stories Transforms Our Lives.* Boston : Beacon Press, 1999. 172.

201 Louise DeSalvo, *Writing as a Way of Healing* 166.

202 James Hillman. *Healing Fiction.*48-49.

203 Amy Tan. "Family Ghosts Hoard Secrets That Bewitch the Living" in *Writers on Writing Volume II: More Collected Essays from The New York Times.* New York: Times Books, Henry Holt, 2003. 244.

204 James W. Pennebaker. "Writing About Emotional Experiences As A Therapeutic Process." *Psychological Science*, Vol. 8, No. 3, May 1997. 162-166.

205 James W. Pennebaker *Opening Up: The Healing Power of Confiding in Others.* (New York: William Morrow, 1990), 42.

206 James W. Pennebaker *Opening Up* 21.

207 James W. Pennebaker. "Writing About Emotional Experiences As A Therapeutic Process." *Psychological Science*, Vol. 8, No. 3, May 1997. 164.

208 Pennebaker, James W. "Mechanisms of Social Constraint." In D.M. Wegner and J.W. Pennebaker (Eds), *Handbook of Mental Control.* (Englewood Cliffs, NJ: Prentice Hall, 1993), 217.

209 J. Kagan,, J.S. Reznick and N. Snidman. "Biological Bases of Childhood Shyness." *Science.* 1988. 240. 169.

210 James W. Pennebaker. "Writing About Emotional Experiences As A Therapeutic Process." *Psychological Science*, Vol. 8, No. 3, May 1997. 164.

211 M.S. Greenberg and A.A. Stone. "Writing About Disclosed Versus Undisclosed Traumas: Immediate and Long-Term Effects On Mood and Health." *Journal of Personality and Social Psychology.* 1992. 63. 75-84.

212 James W. Pennebaker and M.E. Francis. "Cognitive, Emotional, and Language Processes in Disclosure." *Cognition and Emotion.* 1996. 10. 601-626.

213 James W. Pennebaker. "Writing About Emotional Experiences As A Therapeutic Process." *Psychological Science*, Vol. 8, No. 3, May 1997. 165.

214 Robert K. Barnhard. *The Barnhard Concise Dictionary of Etymology.* (New York: H.W.Wilson, 1995), 106.

215 Aaron L.Mishara, qtd in Louise DeSalvo, *Writing as a Way of Healing.* 149.

216 Rothschild, Babette. *The Body Remembers.* New York: W.W. Norton, 2000. 173.

217 Louise DeSalvo. *Writing as a Way of Healing.* 57.

218 Thomas Hale, 24.

219 Qtd in DeSalvo, Louise. *Writing as a Way of Healing: How Telling Our Stories Transforms Our Lives.*Boston : Beacon Press, 1999. 66.

220 Aurora Levins Morales. *Medicine Stories.* 61.

221 Louise DeSalvo. *Writing as a Way of Healing.* 206.

222 Rosaria Champagne, qtd in DeSalvo, 168.

223 DeSalvo, 168.

224 DeSalvo, 167.

225 Aurtur W. Frank, qtd in DeSalvo, Louise. *Writing as a Way of Healing.* 215.

226 Aurora Levins Morales. *Medicine Stories.* 16.

227 Shoshana Felman. "Education and Crisis, or the Vicissitudes of Teaching" in *Trauma: Explorations in Memory.* ed. Cathy Caruth. Baltimore: Johns Hopkins U P, 1995.14.

228 Shoshana Felman. "Education and Crisis, 15.

229 Shoshana Felman. "Education and Crisis, 15.

230 Dori Laub. "Truth and Testimony: The Process and the Struggle" in *Trauma: Explorations in Memory.* Ed. Cathy Caruth. Baltimore: John Hopkins U P, 1995. 61-62.

231 Dori Laub. "Truth and Testimony" 63.

232 Dori Laub. "Truth and Testimony" 73-4.

233 Wendy Doniger. *The Implied Spider: Politics and Theology in Myth.* (New York: Columbia UP, 1998), 55-56.

234 Jill Kerr Conway. *When Memory Speaks: Reflections on Autobiography.* (New York: Knopf, 1998), 6.

235 Amy Tan. *The Opposite of Fate: Memories of a Writing Life.* (New York: Penguin Books, 2003),323.

236 Karen McCarthy Brown. *Mama Lola: A Vodou Priestess in Brooklyn.* (Berkeley: U of California P, 1991), xi.

237   Karen McCarthy Brown. *Mama Lola, xi.*

238   Karen McCarthy Brown. *Mama Lola, xi.*

239   Rosalind Shaw. "Feminist Anthropology and the Gendering of Religious Studies." in *The Insider/Outsider Problem in the Study of Religion: A Reader* Ed. Russell T. Mc Cutcheon. (London & New York: Cassell, 1999), 112.

240   Mary Watkins. *Waking Dreams* (Woodstock, Connecticut: Spring Publications, 1984),190.

241   Mary Watkins. *Waking Dreams,* 190.

242   Amy Tan. *The Opposite of Fate: Memories of a Writing Life.* New York: Penguin Books, 2003.111-112.

243   Amy Tan. *The Opposite of Fate.* 111-112.

244   Amy Tan. *The Opposite of Fate.* 111-112.

245   Henry Corbin. "Mundus Imaginalis or the Imaginary and the Imaginal." *Spring 1972,* 1-19.

246   James Hillman. *Re-Visioning Psychology.* (New York: Harper & Row, 1975), 23.

247   James Hillman. *Re-Visioning Psychology* 23.

248   Robert D. Romanyshyn,. *The Ways of the Heart.* 116.

249   Robert D. Romanyshyn,. *The Ways of the Heart.* 121-123.

250   Virginia Wolff, *A Room of One's Own* 113-14, qtd in Mary Watkins *Invisible Guests: The Development of Imaginal Dialogues.* (Woodstock, Connecticut: Spring Publications, 2000),59.

251   Mary Watkins. *Waking Dreams.* (Woodstock, Connecticut: Spring Publications, 1984), xii.

252   James Hillman. *Re-Visioning Psychology.* (New York: Harper & Row, 1975), 13.

253   James Hillman. *Re-Visioning Psychology.* 13.

254   Flannery O'Connor. *Mystery and Manners.*(New York: Farrar, Straus and Giroux, 1969), 83.

255   Watkins, Mary. *Waking Dreams.* (Woodstock, Connecticut: Spring Publications, 1984),139.

256   Adrienne Rich. "Woman and Bird" in *What is Found There.* (New York: W.W. Norton and Company, 1993), 6.

257   Adrienne Rich. "Woman and Bird" 8.

258   Adrienne Rich. "Woman and Bird" 7.

259   Mary Watkins. *Waking Dreams.* 141.

260   Adrienne Rich. "When We Dead Awaken: Writing as Re-Vision" in *Arts of the Possible.* (New York: Norton, 2001), 20.

261   Mary Watkins. *Waking Dreams,* ix.

262   Mary Watkins. *Waking Dreams.* 99.

263   Robert H. Hopcke, *A Guided Tour of the Collected Works of C.G. Jung.* (Boston: Shambhala, 1999), 34.

264   C.G. Jung. *The Structure and Dynamics of the Psyche.* The Collected Works of C.G. Jung. Trans. by R.C.F. Hull. Vol 8. 2nd ed. Bolligen Series 20. Princeton : Princeton U P, 1969. par.168.

265 Mary Watkins. *Invisible Guests: The Development of Imaginal Dialogues.* (Woodstock, Connecticut: Spring Publications, 2000),1.

266 Mary Watkins. *Invisible Guests.* 122.

267 James Hillman. *Re-Visioning Psychology.* 32.

268 Mary Watkins. *Invisible Guests.* 126.

269 Mary Watkins. *Invisible Guests.* 126.

270 Mary Watkins. *Invisible Guests.* 184.

271 Mary Watkins. *Invisible Guests.* 178.

272 Maxine Hong Kingston. *The Woman Warrior: Memoirs of a Girlhood Among Ghosts.* (New York: Vintage. 1989), 8.

273 Maxine Hong Kingston. *The Woman Warrior.* 16.

274 David L. Miller, *Hells and Holy Ghosts.* (Nashville, Tennessee: Abingdon Press, 1989),130-32.

275 John Mbiti. *African Religions and Philosophy.* (New York: Anchor), 28-29.

276 D.T. Naine. S*undiata: An Epic of Old Mali.* Trans. G.D. Pickett. (Harlow, Essex, England: Longman, 1979),87.

277 Grace Lewis McLaren. "The Mythos Quartet: A Hermeneutical Exploration of Four Ancestral Voices." Dissertation. Pacifica Graduate Institute: Carpinteria, California 2000. iv.

278 Kent Haruf. "Writers on Writing; To See Your Story Clearly, Start by Pulling the Wool Over Your Own Eyes." *New York Times on the Web*, November 20, 2000. June 12, 2002 <http://query.nytimes.com/search/restricted/article?res=F10A16F8355FOC738EDDA80994D8404. par.6-7.

279 Amy Tan. *The Opposite of Fate: Memories of a Writing Life.* New York: Penguin Books, 2003. 36.

www.ingramcontent.com/pod-product-compliance
Lightning Source LLC
Chambersburg PA
CBHW061404280526
45784CB00001B/367